Workbook

Economics with Emphasis on the Free Enterprise System

T0325357

Irvin B. Tucker
University of North Carolina-Charlotte

Joan S. Ryan
Clackamas Community College
Portland, Oregon

⁂ Cengage

Australia • Brazil • Canada • Mexico • Singapore • United Kingdom • United States

For product information and technology assistance, contact us at
**Cengage Customer & Sales Support, 1-800-354-9706
or support.cengage.com.**

For permission to use material from this text or product, submit all requests online at **www.copyright.com.**

ISBN-13: 978-1-133-59340-9

Cengage
5191 Natorp Boulevard
Mason, OH 45040
USA

Cengage is a leading provider of customized learning solutions. Our employees reside in nearly 40 different countries and serve digital learners in 165 countries around the world. Find your local representative at: **www.cengage.com.**

For your course and learning solutions, visit **www.cengage.com/school.**

Visit our company website at **www.cengage.com.**

Printed Number: 2   Print Year: 2024
Printed in Mexico

Table of Contents

UNIT 3   BUSINESS IN ACTION

Chapter 6   Business Organizations

Chapter 7   Business Ownership

UNIT 4   MONEY AND BANKING

Chapter 8   Money and the Banking System

Chapter 9   Financial Institutions and Markets

Chapter 10   Consumer Credit and Debt

UNIT 5   MEASURING ECONOMIC PERFORMANCE

Chapter 11 Gross Domestic Product and Economic Growth

Chapter 12 Challenges to Free Enterprise

UNIT 6   GOVERNMENT IN THE MACRO ECONOMY

Chapter 13 Government Spending and Taxing

Chapter 14 Federal Reserve and Monetary Policy

UNIT 7   THE GLOBAL TRADE AND INVESTING

Chapter 15 International Trade

Chapter 16 Build Assets and Wealth

Chapter 17 Invest for the Future

1-1 What Is Free Enterprise?

Part 1 True or False

Directions: Place a *T* for True or an *F* for False in the Answers column to show whether each of the following statements is true or false.

Answers

1. In a free enterprise system, consumers and businesses buy and sell products with a minimum of government restrictions. **LO 1-1** 1._____

2. The economic problem of *scarcity* does not exist for the wealthy. **LO 1-1** 2._____

3. Resources are the basic categories of inputs used to produce goods and services. **LO 1-2** 3._____

4. A *manager* is a business leader who seeks to make profits by combining resources to produce new goods and services. **LO 1-2** 4._____

5. All nations have the same ability to produce goods and services. **LO 1-2** 5._____

6. Coal, diamonds, and oil are examples of capital. **LO 1-2** 6._____

7. The labor resource is measured by the number of people available for work. **LO 1-2** 7._____

8. Scarcity forces people to make choices. **LO 1-3** 8._____

9. Microeconomics studies decision making for the economy as a whole. **LO 1-3** 9._____

10. Economists are not concerned with the economic decisions individuals make. **LO 1-3** 10._____

Part 2 Multiple Choice

Directions: In the Answers column, write the letter that represents the word, or group of words, that correctly completes the statement or answers the question.

Answers

11. Any place or method used by buyers and sellers to exchange goods and services is called _____. (a) a business (b) a market (c) entrepreneurship (d) free enterprise **LO 1-1** 11._____

12. Which of the following is a hallmark of free enterprise? (a) a minimum of government restriction (b) the use of legal tender (c) strong labor unions (d) high unemployment **LO 1-1** 12._____

13. "You can't have it all" is a good way to describe the economic problem of _____. (a) inefficiency (b) inflation (c) poverty (d) scarcity **LO 1-1** 13._____

14. Resources are sometimes called _____. (a) factors of production (b) economic variables (c) real property (d) wealth **LO 1-2** 14._____

15. Which of the following would be considered an example of land? (a) forests (b) wind (c) coal (d) all of these **LO 1-2** 15._____

16. Which of the following is *not* considered a basic category of input used to produce goods and services? (a) land (b) labor (c) real estate (d) capital **LO 1-2** 16._____

17. Which of these is an example of capital? (a) a 100-acre field on the outskirts of town (b) a factory that sits on the 100-acre field (c) the 200 workers employed at the factory (d) the individual who owns and operates the factory **LO 1-2** 17._____

18. *Economics* is best defined as the study of _____. (a) fluctuations in the stock market and   18._____
the variables that cause them (b) monetary decisions that affect individuals rather than society
at large (c) how society chooses to use its scarce resources for the production of goods and
services to satisfy unlimited wants (d) the ever-changing forces of supply and demand **LO 1-3**

19. Which of these is an example of microeconomic analysis? (a) examining how a specific   19._____
company can maximize its production and capacity so it can lower prices and better compete
in the marketplace (b) making economic statements based on value judgments (c) studying the
effect that federal tax cuts will have on unemployment (d) all of these **LO 1-3**

20. It is fair to say that macroeconomics _____. (a) examines the economy from the "bottom   20._____
up" (b) is most concerned about economic decisions made by individuals (c) takes a "big
picture" approach to the economy (d) tells us more about specific markets than
microeconomics **LO 1-3**

Part 3 Short Answer

Directions: Read the following questions, and write your response.

21. Explain what causes the economic effect of *scarcity*. What does the condition of scarcity cause in turn?
LO 1-1/LO 1-3

22. Name two factors used to measure the labor resource. **LO 1-2**

Part 4 Critical Thinking

Directions: Read the following question, and write your response.

23. In the space below, identify the three basic categories of resources used to produce goods and services.
Then, think about a carton of orange juice and all the resources that went into making it. For each
category of resource you have listed, give at least two specific examples that were used to produce the
carton of juice. **LO 1-2**

1-2 Principles and Goals of Free Enterprise

Part 1 True or False

Directions: Place a *T* for True or an *F* for False in the Answers column to show whether each of the following statements is true or false.

Answers

1. Private property rights allow individuals and groups to own businesses and resources. **LO 2-1**   1._____

2. The major reason people start a new business is to provide needed goods to society. **LO 2-1**   2._____

3. Competition is not a major component of the free enterprise system. **LO 2-1**   3._____

4. Self-interest is discouraged in the free enterprise system. **LO 2-1**   4._____

5. Personal economic freedoms include the right to make one's own economic choices. **LO 2-2**   5._____

6. Social Security benefits help encourage the economic goal of full employment and stable prices. **LO 2-2**   6._____

7. The *What question* requires an economy to decide the mix and quantity of goods and services that it will produce. **LO 2-2**   7._____

8. The *How question* asks whether production will be more or less capital-intensive. **LO 2-3**   8._____

9. In a free enterprise system, the government answers the three fundamental economic questions. **LO 2-3**   9._____

10. The free enterprise system uses price to decide who will receive the goods and services that are produced. **LO 2-3**   10._____

Part 2 Multiple Choice

Directions: In the Answers column, write the letter that represents the word, or group of words, that correctly completes the statement or answers the question.

Answers

11. Which of the following is an example of public property? (a) Yellowstone National Park (b) the Microsoft Corporation (c) Disneyworld (d) the song "Rolling in the Deep," by Adele **LO 2-1**   11._____

12. The federal government has taken some land that belongs to Thomas in order to build a new highway. As directed by the Constitution, the government pays Thomas "just compensation" for taking his land. Which principle of the free enterprise system is involved here? (a) the profit motive (b) competition (c) private property rights (d) freedom of choice **LO 2-1**   12._____

13. The freedom of individuals to cast their dollar votes to buy, or not buy, at prices set in competitive markets is called _____. (a) opportunity cost (b) competition (c) consumer sovereignty (d) self-interest **LO 2-1**   13._____

14. Which of the following statements correctly explains the concept of *voluntary exchange*? (a) profitable businesses must face the rivalry of other businesses (b) buyers and sellers decide what to buy and sell with a minimum of government intervention (c) consumers signal what products businesses should offer for sale (d) entrepreneurs start new businesses mainly to make a profit **LO 2-1**   14._____

15. Producing the most goods and services from limited resources is _____. (a) economic freedom (b) the profit motive (c) consumer sovereignty (d) economic efficiency **LO 2-2**   15._____

16. Economic equity decides _____. (a) how the economic pie is divided (b) the price you   16._____
    will pay for products (c) that income should be provided only to those who directly contribute
    to production (d) that everyone who wants a job will have one **LO 2-2**

17. Which economic goal is most closely connected to improving the standard of living?   17._____
    (a) economic growth (b) economic freedom (c) economic efficiency (d) economic security
    LO 2-2

18. The Employment Act of 1946 addressed the economic goal of _____. (a) freedom of   18._____
    choice (b) full employment (c) economic growth (d) competition **LO 2-2**

19. Every economy must answer the *What question* because of _____. (a) economic equity   19._____
    (b) voluntary exchange (c) economic security (d) the problem of scarcity **LO 2-3**

20. Which of the following is an example of a *How question*? (a) Should we produce electricity   20._____
    from coal or nuclear energy? (b) Should we manufacture flags or tents? (c) What price should
    we charge for this Smartphone? (d) Should we market our bicycles to families or sports
    enthusiasts? **LO 2-3**

Part 3 Short Answer

Directions: Read the following questions, and write your response.

21. Describe at least three personal economic freedoms that you enjoy. **LO 2-2**

22. What is the role of education in answering the *How question*? **LO 2-3**

Part 4 Critical Thinking

Directions: Read the following question, and write your response.

23. Suppose your community passes a law banning showers and toilets that use too much water. In the space
    below, indicate whether you believe the law supports or does not support the five main principles of free
    enterprise. Then tell whether you would support such a law. Explain your answer. **LO 2-1**

1-3 Types of Economic Systems

Part 1 True or False

Directions: Place a *T* for True or an *F* for False in the Answers column to show whether each of the following statements is true or false.

Answers

1. An economic system involves the methods used to answer the *What, How,* and *For Whom* questions. **LO 3-1** — 1._____

2. Traditional economies exist today only in undeveloped or Third World countries. **LO 3-1** — 2._____

3. A major benefit of a traditional economy is that it reduces friction among members. **LO 3-1** — 3._____

4. A market economy answers the basic economic questions based only on voluntary buying and selling in the marketplace. **LO 3-1** — 4._____

5. Competition regulates the economy in a free enterprise system. **LO 3-1** — 5._____

6. Adam Smith and Milton Friedman are best known for their strong championing of command economies. **LO 3-1** — 6._____

7. Capitalism is an economic system based on government ownership of resources and centralized decision making. **LO 3-1** — 7._____

8. In a perfect communist society, there is no government and all resources are owned by the workers. **LO 3-1** — 8._____

9. In the real world, no nation is a pure traditional, command, or market economy. **LO 3-2** — 9._____

10. The act of transforming a private enterprise into a government enterprise is called *socialization.* **LO 3-2** — 10._____

Part 2 Multiple Choice

Directions: In the Answers column, write the letter that represents the word, or group of words, that correctly completes the statement or answers the question.

Answers

11. The Amish of Pennsylvania and the Inuit of Canada use this type of economy. (a) market (b) traditional (c) mixed (d) command **LO 3-1** — 11._____

12. A common criticism of traditional economies is that (a) they lead to intense competition among members (b) wealth is almost always inequitably distributed (c) personal greed is rampant and widespread (d) they do not produce advanced goods or high standards of living **LO 3-1** — 12._____

13. What did Adam Smith mean when he said the market economy is guided by an "invisible hand"? (a) government control over the economy leads to the best outcome for all (b) copying the previous generation is the best way to structure an economy (c) the best interests of society are served by markets guided by self-interest (d) the profit motive should have no impact on our economic choices **LO 3-1** — 13._____

14. This economic system is based on private ownership of resources and markets. (a) socialism (b) barter (c) capitalism (d) communism **LO 3-1** — 14._____

15. "From each according to his ability, to each according to his need" was a key principle underlying the views of _____. (a) Karl Marx (b) Adam Smith (c) Milton Friedman (d) Friedrich von Hayek **LO 3-1** — 15._____

16. In a command economy, the basic economic questions are answered by _____. 16._____
    (a) entrepreneurs (b) a dictator or central authority (c) custom and tradition (d) buyers and sellers **LO 3-1**

17. Communists reject the concept of _____. (a) private property (b) the profit motive 17._____
    (c) self-interest (d) all of these **LO 3-1**

18. Which of the following nations have an economy that is closest to pure socialism? (a) China 18._____
    (b) North Korea (c) Sweden (d) South Korea **LO 3-2**

19. The U.S. government collects taxes from citizens to fund government programs. This 19._____
    indicates that _____. (a) the U.S. economy contains elements of the command system
    (b) there is no real economic freedom in the U.S. (c) the United States is a pure command
    economy (d) economic growth is not important to most U.S. lawmakers **LO 3-2**

20. Which of the following is an example of *nationalization*? (a) the 2008 bankruptcy of Circuit 20._____
    City electronics stores (b) the 1974 filing of an antitrust lawsuit by the U.S. Department of
    Justice against AT&T (c) the establishment of the Resolution Trust Corporation in 1989
    (d) all of these **LO 3-2**

Part 3 Short Answer

Directions: Read the following questions, and write your response.

21. Identify one advantage and one disadvantage of a traditional economy. **LO 3-1**

22. Why would Adam Smith likely not be troubled by income inequity in a society? **LO 3-1**

23. Though the U.S. is best characterized as a market economy, it contains elements of traditional and
    command economies as well. Identify one element of each of these two systems that is present in the
    U.S. economy. **LO 3-2**

Part 4 Critical Thinking

Directions: Read the following question, and write your response.

24. In the space below, write one paragraph about of the economic system in place in the United States today
    through the eyes of either Adam Smith or Karl Marx. What does he admire about the U.S. economy?
    What does he dislike? Provide explanations for your response. **LO 3-1/LO 3-2**

Chapter 1 Review

Part 1 True or False

Directions: Place a *T* for True or an *F* for False in the Answers column to show whether each of the following statements is true or false.

Answers

1. In the free enterprise system, both consumers and businesses benefit from exchange. **LO 1-1**   1._____

2. The problem of scarcity affects individuals only, not governments or businesses. **LO 1-1**   2._____

3. The three *factors of production* are competition, private property ownership, and the profit motive. **LO 1-2**   3._____

4. Money is not considered capital because in-and-of itself it produces nothing. **LO 1-2**   4._____

5. Macroeconomics studies the economic decisions made by individual businesses. **LO 1-3**   5._____

6. One reason why highly regulated economies have poor economic performance is that they frequently eliminate the profit motive. **LO 2-1**   6._____

7. Economic security means producing the most goods and services from limited resources. **LO 2-2**   7._____

8. The *For whom* question means that society must have a way to decide who will be wealthy and who will be poor. **LO 2-3**   8._____

9. The basis of the command system is capitalism. **LO 3-1**   9._____

10. The U.S. economy is best characterized as a pure free enterprise system. **LO 3-2**   10._____

Part 2 Multiple Choice

Directions: In the Answers column, write the letter that represents the word, or group of words, that correctly completes the statement or answers the question.

Answers

11. The economic problem of scarcity exists for _____. (a) everyone but the very wealthy (b) individuals but not society as a whole (c) only those who live in less-developed countries (d) all individuals, societies, and governments—whether rich or poor **LO 1-1**   11._____

12. The services of farmers, airline pilots, teachers, and coal miners are all examples of _____. (a) labor (b) capital (c) entrepreneurship (d) the "invisible hand" **LO 1-2**   12._____

13. Examining the effect of an oil spill on the national average of consumer prices is an example of _____. (a) marginal analysis (b) cost-benefit (c) macroeconomic analysis (d) microeconomic analysis **LO 1-3**   13._____

14. Economic competition _____. (a) results in a great variety of goods and services (b) is a hallmark of the free enterprise system (c) forces businesses to offer better products at lower prices (d) all of these **LO 2-1**   14._____

15. Economic equity concerns which of the following questions? (a) Is a job available in the system for everyone who wants one? (b) What products will be produced? (c) Should I purchase this product or a product from another business? (d) Is there an equal opportunity for each person to participate in and benefit from the system? **LO 2-2**   15._____

16. In a command economy, the *How question* is answered by _____ . (a) the government   16._____
    (b) the consumer (c) the producer (d) tradition **LO 2-3/LO 3-1**

17. Which of the following is *not* one of the three basic types of economic systems? (a) market   17._____
    (b) command (c) competitive (d) traditional **LO 3-1**

18. Which of the following is a common criticism of market economies? (a) lack of individual   18._____
    initiative (b) inhibits advancement of technology (c) results in low productivity (d) generates
    wealth inequality **LO 3-1**

19. All of the following concepts are associated with Adam Smith *except* (a) laissez faire   19._____
    (b) class struggle (c) the invisible hand (d) self-interest **LO 3-1**

20. A _____ economy is a system that answers the three basic economic questions through   20._____
    a combination of traditional, command, and market systems. (a) competitive (b) mixed
    (c) socialist (d) capitalist **LO 3-2**

Part 3 Short Answer

Directions: Read the following questions, and write your response.

21. Give an example of a question that would be answered by macroeconomic analysis and a question that
    would be answered by microeconomic analysis. **LO 1-3**

22. Identify the three fundamental economic questions. Explain how the U.S. economy answers each
    question. **LO 2-3/LO 3-1**

Part 4 Critical Thinking

Directions: Read the following question, and write your response.

23. Indicate whether you think each of the following activities is *most* likely to occur in a traditional,
    command, or market economy. **LO 3-1**

    a. A coffee shop owner decides to lower the price of the lattes she serves in her store by 25 cents; when
       a competitor learns about the lower price, he reduces his price also.

    b. A community of farmers uses plows harnessed to oxen to plant crops, making sure to rotate the fields
       just the way their fathers and grandfathers did.

    c. On the day the latest video game system is released, people stand in long lines at toy stores hoping to
       snag one before they sell out. Because demand is high and supply is low, the stores are doubling the
       price of the system—and people are gladly paying!

    d. The government decides to reduce production at domestic oil refineries in order to decrease the
       available supply.

2-1 The Economist's Toolkit

Part 1 True or False

Directions: Place a *T* for True or an *F* for False in the Answers column to show whether each of the following statements is true or false.

Answers

1. Economists use a step-by-step method for solving problems. **LO 1-1**   1._____

2. A *model* is a simplification of reality used to understand the relationship between variables. **LO 1-1**   2._____

3. All economic models are useful, whether or not they yield accurate predictions. **LO 1-1**   3._____

4. A graph is the simplest way to present and understand the relationship between economic variables. **LO 1-2**   4._____

5. Basic economic analysis concerns the relationship among three or more variables. **LO 1-2**   5._____

6. A two-variable graph assumes all other variables not shown in the graph are unchanged. **LO 1-2**   6._____

7. When the price of computer tablets is low, consumers purchase a greater quantity of them. This is an example of a direct relationship. **LO 1-2**   7._____

8. When two events occur at the same time, this is called *causation*. **LO 1-2**   8._____

9. Positive economics is an analysis based on facts. **LO 1-3**   9._____

10. When using value judgments, an economist's arguments may have no more value than others' arguments. **LO 1-3**   10._____

Part 2 Multiple Choice

Directions: In the Answers column, write the letter that represents the word, or group of words, that correctly completes the statement or answers the question.

Answers

11. What is the first step in the model-building process? (a) develop a theory (b) build a model (c) make an assumption (d) identify the problem **LO 1-1**   11._____

12. _____ is another name for *model*. (a) Theory (b) Assumption (c) Hypothesis (d) Axiom **LO 1-1**   12._____

13. Which of the following statements about a model is correct? (a) Models make the relationship between variables difficult to understand. (b) A model assumes that all variables being studied are constantly changing. (c) A model must include an assumption. (d) All of the statements are true. **LO 1-1**   13._____

14. An assumption is _____. (a) a simplification of reality used to understand the relationship between variables (b) something that is accepted as being true (c) an educated guess about economic conditions (d) an economic principle that has been proven accurate **LO 1-1**   14._____

15. Which of the following is an example of a direct relationship? (a) as income falls, personal debt increases (b) as price falls, sales rise (c) as income rises, expenses increase (d) as hours worked rise, leisure time decreases **LO 1-2**   15._____

16. In this kind of relationship, both variables change in the same direction. (a) direct relationship (b) negative relationship (c) inverse relationship (d) causative relationship **LO 1-2**   16._____

17. When the price of steak is high, consumers buy less steak. This is an example of which type of relationship? (a) normative (b) direct (c) positive (d) inverse **LO 1-2** 17._____

18. Correlation occurs when _____. (a) one event causes another to happen (b) variables move in the same direction (c) two events happen at the same time (d) variables move in the opposite direction **LO 1-2** 18._____

19. Positive analysis _____. (a) uses statements that can be proven either true or false (b) is based on value judgments (c) often uses words such as *need* and *should* (d) is always accurate **LO 1-3** 19._____

20. Which of the following statements is an example of normative analysis? (a) If the unemployment rate rises to 9 percent, then teenage unemployment exceeds 80 percent. (b) When the minimum wage rises by 50 cents, unemployment rises by 1 percent. (c) Too many countries are still poor and need more productive resources. (d) All are examples of normative analysis. **LO 1-3** 20._____

Part 3 Short Answer

Directions: Read the following questions, and write your response.

21. Identify the three steps in the model-building process. Explain why the third step is so important. **LO 1-1**

22. Use your own experiences to provide an example of a direct economic relationship and an inverse economic relationship. **LO 1-2**

Part 4 Critical Thinking

Directions: Read the following question, and write your response.

23. Identify the following statements as either positive or normative analysis. **LO 1-3**

- The gasoline tax unfairly penalizes motorists, particularly low-income drivers. _____
- A rise in consumer incomes will lead to a rise in the demand for new cars. _____
- The national minimum wage should be increased by $2.00 per hour to reduce poverty. _____
- The government is right to introduce a ban on smoking in public places. _____
- If the exchange rate falls, we will see an increase in exports overseas. _____
- A reduction in corporate taxes will result in an increase in the number of people hired. _____
- The retirement age should be raised to 72 to combat the effects of our aging population. _____
- If the government bans smoking in public places, the income of restaurants will fall. _____
- Fair weather in the summer will increase the demand for barbecue grills. _____

2-2 Opportunity Cost

Part 1 True or False

Directions: Place a *T* for True or an *F* for False in the Answers column to show whether each of the following statements is true or false.

Answers

1. Everyday decisions involve trade-offs. **LO 2-1**   1._____

2. Because of scarcity, the three basic economic questions cannot be answered without sacrifice   2._____
    or cost. **LO 2-1**

3. Economists define *cost* as simply the purchase price of a good or service. **LO 2-1**   3._____

4. Making rational consumer choices can be done without time and information. **LO 2-1**   4._____

5. *Opportunity cost* is the value of all the options given up when a decision is made. **LO 2-1**   5._____

6. The concept of opportunity cost applies only to consumer decisions, and not to those made by   6._____
    business and government. **LO 2-1**

7. Most economic decisions involve marginal analysis. **LO 2-2**   7._____

8. *Marginal benefit* is the extra cost from an additional unit of change. **LO 2-2**   8._____

9. If a business is offered a deal in which marginal benefit is less than marginal cost, the   9._____
    business should make the deal. **LO 2-2**

10. In the long run, any firm that does not follow the cost-benefit rule will go out of business.   10._____
    LO 2-2

Part 2 Multiple Choice

Directions: In the Answers column, write the letter that represents the word, or group of words, that correctly completes the statement or answers the question.

Answers

11. A trade-off is _____. (a) the value of the next best option sacrificed for a chosen option   11._____
    (b) all the options given up when a decision is made (c) the price of not choosing the best
    alternative (d) the decision about how much more or less to do **LO 2-1**

12. Which of the following decisions involve a trade-off? (a) You decide to take a part-time job   12._____
    at the library rather than at the zoo. (b) A farmer decides to plant strawberries rather than
    raspberries. (c) A school district decides to cancel all field trips for the year to stay under
    budget, rather than lay off several teachers. (d) All of these decisions involve trade-offs.
    LO 2-1

13. The value of the next best option sacrificed for a chosen option is the _____. (a) true cost   13._____
    (b) opportunity cost (c) marginal benefit (d) marginal cost **LO 2-1**

14. Which of the following statements is true of opportunity cost? (a) It is the value of all   14._____
    alternatives you pass up when you make a choice. (b) It is the value of the next best
    alternative you give up when you make a choice. (c) It can only be measured in dollar terms.
    (d) It is the same for all individuals. **LO 2-1**

15. Sally, a baker, decides to go back to school to become a lawyer. In this case, the opportunity   15._____
    cost is _____. (a) the rent Sally no longer pays on the bakery (b) the clients who will
    receive legal counsel from Sally when she passes the bar (c) the baked goods Sally no longer
    provides (d) the cost of tuition Sally pays for law school **LO 2-1**

16. Suppose you are deciding to major in economics, English, or philosophy. It is a close call   16._____
    between economics and English, but economics wins out. In this case, the opportunity cost of
    choosing to be an economics major is (a) being an English major (b) the price you will pay
    for economics textbooks (c) being an English major or philosophy major (d) the income you
    will earn as a professional economist **LO 2-1**

17. The decision about how much more or less to do is _____ (a) marginal analysis   17._____
    (b) inverse analysis (c) positive analysis (d) normative analysis **LO 2-2**

18. When you use marginal analysis to make decisions, you are _____. (a) making   18._____
    assumptions (b) thinking at the margin (c) practicing the model-building process (d) thinking
    outside the box **LO 2-2**

19. The extra gain from an additional unit of change is _____. (a) opportunity cost   19._____
    (b) net benefit (c) marginal benefit (d) positive gain **LO 2-2**

20. Which of the following compares the additional rewards and costs of an action to determine   20._____
    if the benefits outweigh the costs? (a) cost-benefit analysis (b) normative analysis (c) positive
    analysis (d) theoretical analysis **LO 2-2**

Part 3 Short Answer

Directions: Read the following questions, and write your response.

21. Describe an opportunity cost and a trade-off about your decision to brown-bag your lunch today. **LO 2-1**

22. How does one determine net benefit? **LO 2-2**

Part 4 Critical Thinking

Directions: Read the following question, and write your response.

23. Following is a cost-benefit analysis of (A) attending a local college or (B) attending out-of-state college

Create two cost-benefit grids to analyze a decision you have to make. Assign weights to each quadrant based on how important each cost or benefit is to you (1 being not important, 5 being very important). Add your columns and analyze your results. Does this help you with your decision? Why or why not? **LO 2-2**

A Attend local college		B Attend out-of-state college	
Costs	Benefits	Cost	Benefits

2-3 Production Possibilities Curve

Part 1 True or False

Directions: Place a *T* for True or an *F* for False in the Answers column to show whether each of the following statements is true or false.

Answers

1. Scarcity means that society's capacity to produce is limited. **LO 3-1**   1. _____
2. The production possibilities curve does not allow an economy to shift a resource from producing one output to producing another. **LO 3-1**   2. _____
3. Any point *inside* the production possibilities curve indicates efficiency. **LO 3-1**   3. _____
4. Any point *outside* the production possibilities curve is impossible. **LO 3-1**   4. _____
5. Opportunity costs can be explained with a PPC graph. **LO 3-2**   5. _____
6. As more of an economy's resources are devoted to producing Product A, even greater quantities of production of Product B must be given up. **LO 3-2**   6. _____
7. All resources are equally suited to all types of production. The problem is simply deciding what to produce with the available resources. **LO 3-2**   7. _____
8. An economy's production capacity is always fixed. **LO 3-3**   8. _____
9. There is only one way to achieve economic growth: to gain resources. **LO 3-3**   9. _____
10. Technological change can result from entrepreneurship. **LO 3-3**   10. _____

Part 2 Multiple Choice

Directions: In the Answers column, write the letter that represents the word, or group of words, that correctly completes the statement or answers the question.

Answers

11. The production possibilities curve shows _____ (a) each trade-off made by an economy (b) the effect of unemployment on production (c) the maximum possible output for an economy (d) the total dollar cost of all economic choices made **LO 3-1**   11. _____
12. The production possibilities curve model assumes that _____. (a) natural resources do not increase (b) capital grows along with production (c) technology is never fixed (d) labor cannot be transferred from one task to another **LO 3-1**   12. _____
13. The body of knowledge applied to how goods and services are produced is called _____. (a) entrepreneurship (b) capital (c) technology (d) human resources **LO 3-1**   13. _____
14. Producing the maximum output with given resources and technology is called _____. (a) rational self-interest (b) productivity (c) efficiency (d) opportunity cost **LO 3-1**   14. _____
15. Which of the following statements about the PPC is correct? (a) All points inside the PPC are unattainable. (b) All points on the curve are efficient. (c) All points outside the curve are underutilization points. (d) Each PPC identifies only one single point of efficiency. **LO 3-1**   15. _____
16. This occurs when an economy fails to use its resources fully. (a) trade-offs (b) sunk costs (c) scarcity (d) underutilization **LO 3-1**   16. _____
17. A PPC shows radio production along the vertical axis and TV production along the horizontal axis. At the point where the PPC touches the horizontal axis, _____ are produced (a) no radios (b) no TVs (c) the maximum number of radios and TVs (d) no radios *or* TVs **LO 3-2**   17. _____

18. The law of increasing opportunity cost states that _____. (a) opportunity cost is irrelevant   18. _____
(b) opportunity cost increases as production of an output expands (c) any point outside the
PPC is unattainable (d) there is no limit to the quantity of goods and services an economy can
produce **LO 3-2**

19. The ability of an economy to produce greater levels of output is called _____. (a) net   19. _____
benefit (b) productivity (c) efficiency (d) economic growth **LO 3-2**

20. Which of these is *not* a source of technological change? (a) inventions (b) entrepreneurship   20. _____
(c) increasing the number of workers (d) new knowledge **LO 3-3**

Part 3 Short Answer

Directions: Read the following questions, and write your response.

21. What is the effect of high unemployment on the PPC? **LO 3-1**

22. True or False: All points along the PPC are points of maximum efficiency. Explain your answer.
LO 3-1

23. A company hires 50 additional employees and installs a new, more efficient computer system. What is
the likely effect on the PPC? **LO 3-3**

Part 4 Critical Thinking

Directions: Read the following question, and write your response.

24. In the space below, graph the following production possibility alternatives: Alternative A—300 MP3
players, 0 cell phones; Alternative B—270 MP3 players, 10 cell phones; Alternative C—215 MP3
players, 20 cell phones; Alternative D—135 MP3 players, 30 cell phones; Alternative E—0 MP3
players, 40 cell phones **LO 3-1**

25. Describe the effect you think Bill Gates and Microsoft Corporation have had on the PPC. **LO 3-3**

Chapter 2 Review

Part 1 True or False

Directions: Place a *T* for True or an *F* for False in the Answers column to show whether each of the following statements is true or false.

Answers

1. A model emphasizes those variables that are most important by assuming that all other variables remain unchanged. **LO 1-1**
  1. ____

2. A graph is the only way economists describe economic information. **LO 1-2**
  2. ____

3. The law of demand is a direct relationship between price and demand. **LO 1-2**
  3. ____

4. A positive economic statement is not necessarily correct. **LO 1-3**
  4. ____

5. Very wealthy people never need to make trade-offs. **LO 2-1**
  5. ____

6. When making an economic decision, the opportunity cost of the chosen item or activity is the value of the next best alternative you must pass up. **LO 2-1**
  6. ____

7. Rational decision makers decide on an option only if its marginal cost is greater than its marginal benefit. **LO 2-2**
  7. ____

8. The PPC assumes that technology is fixed or unchanged. **LO 3-1**
  8. ____

9. Opportunity cost rises as production of an output expands. **LO 3-2**
  9. ____

10. Economic growth occurs when the PPC shifts inward. **LO 3-2**
  10. ____

Part 2 Multiple Choice

Directions: In the Answers column, write the letter that represents the word, or group of words, that correctly completes the statement or answers the question.

Answers

11. Economic models _____. (a) determine how the economy will behave in the year to come (b) influence how goods and services are produced (c) make predictions about the economy (d) completely explain in detail why certain trends occur **LO 1-1**
  11. ____

12. Which of the statements is correct if there is a *positive* relationship between education and annual income? (a) The more education you have, the lower your annual income. (b) The more education you have, the higher your annual income. (c) Education has little impact on annual income. (d) People with higher annual incomes attend more expensive schools than people with lower incomes. **LO 1-2**
  12. ____

13. Normative statements _____. (a) are based on facts (b) are testable (c) express an opinion (d) are always accurate **LO 1-3**
  13. ____

14. If you decide to study for an upcoming test instead of going to the movies, what must you take into account? (a) sunk cost (b) economic theory (c) opportunity cost (d) scarcity **LO 2-1**
  14. ____

15. What does cost-benefit analysis do? (a) makes a positive prediction about an economic event (b) shows a negative relationship between two variables (c) makes the relationship between variables easier to understand (d) compares the additional rewards and costs of an action to determine if the benefits outweigh the costs **LO 2-2**
  15. ____

16. Walter has decided to hire a new employee at his candy store. Walter has concluded that (a) the cost of hiring employees has increased (b) the benefit of hiring employees has decreased (c) the marginal benefit of hiring a new employee exceeds its marginal cost (d) the marginal cost of hiring a new employee exceeds its marginal benefit **LO 2-2**

16. ____

17. The maximum possible output for an economy is shown by (a) the production possibilities curve (b) cost-benefit analysis (c) marginal analysis (d) economic models **LO 3-1**

17. ____

18. The PPC assumes which of the following resources remains fixed? (a) land (b) labor (c) capital (d) all of the choices are fixed resources **LO 3-1**

18. ____

19. All points along the PPC _____. (a) are inefficient (b) illustrate maximum output levels (c) are underutilization points (d) are unattainable **LO 3-1**

19. ____

20. Any _____ in resources shifts the production possibilities curve _____. (a) increase; inward (b) increase; outward (c) decrease; vertically (d) decrease; horizontally **LO 3-3**

20. ____

Part 3 Short Answer

Directions: Read the following questions, and write your response.

21. What impact has increasing immigration to the United States had on the PPC? Explain your answer. **LO 3-3**

22. Suppose you exercise five times a week and are thinking about adding a sixth day to your routine. Perform marginal analysis to determine whether you will add the sixth day. **LO 2-2**

Part 4 Critical Thinking

Directions: Read the following question, and write your response.

23. Indicate whether you think each of the following relationships is either direct or inverse. Explain your answers. **LO 1-2**

   a. Inches of snow and snow shovels purchased

   b. Price of computer tablet and quantity purchased

   c. Price of hamburger and sales of hamburger buns

   d. Annual income and amount of mortgage on residence

3-1 The Law of Demand

Part 1 True or False

Directions: Place a *T* for True or an *F* for False in the Answers column to show whether each of the following statements is true or false.

Answers

1. In a market, demand is the selling side. **LO 1-1**
   1._____

2. In a free enterprise system, consumers serve their best interest by buying at the lowest price. **LO 1-1**
   2._____

3. A demand schedule lists the quantity of a good or service consumers purchase at various possible prices. **LO 1-1**
   3._____

4. By moving along the demand curve, you can find the quantity a seller will offer at any possible selling price. **LO 1-1**
   4._____

5. The demand curve is a summary of a consumer's buying intentions. **LO 1-1**
   5._____

6. Economists can calculate demand curves for individuals, but not for entire markets. **LO 1-2**
   6._____

7. Individual demand curves are the same for all consumers. **LO 1-2**
   7._____

8. The law of demand applies both to individuals and to entire markets. **LO 1-2**
   8._____

9. When price rises, the quantity demanded by a market goes down. **LO 1-2**
   9._____

10. Unlike the individual demand curve, the assumption for market demand is that all variables are changing constantly. **LO 1-2**
    10._____

Part 2 Multiple Choice

Directions: In the Answers column, write the letter that represents the word, or group of words, that correctly completes the statement or answers the question.

Answers

11. Demand is the relationship between _____ and _____, when other variables are held constant. (a) supply, price (b) price, quantity demanded (c) quality, price (d) supply, quantity demanded **LO 1-1**
    11._____

12. What is *quantity demanded*? (a) the amount of goods and services purchased at a given price (b) the amount of goods and services supplied by producers at any given time (c) the amount of goods and services available at a given price (d) the amount of goods and services that would be purchased if price were reduced **LO 1-1**
    12._____

13. The law of demand states that there is a(n) _____ relationship between price and quantity demanded. (a) direct (b) neutral (c) positive (d) inverse **LO 1-1**
    13._____

14. The manager of a sandwich shop has decided to lower prices this week on all sandwiches by one dollar. If the law of demand is correct, which of the following will *most likely* occur? (a) there will be little change in the number of sandwiches the shop sells this week (b) the manager will lay off some employees this week (c) the shop will have more customers this week than last week (d) it will be a slow week in the shop this week **LO 1-1**
    14._____

15. A demand schedule for Adele's latest CD would show _____. (a) various prices of the CD (b) quantity demanded of the CD (c) both a and b (d) neither a nor b **LO 1-1**
    15._____

16. Which statement about demand curves is *incorrect*? (a) demand curves can be calculated for goods but not for services (b) the demand curve is formed by connecting points that represent possible combinations of price and quantity purchased by consumers (c) the demand curve can tell you how many items a buyer will purchase (d) demand curves assume that other variables are held constant **LO 1-1**   16._____

17. Which of the following accurately summarizes the law of demand? (a) as prices rise, quantity demanded increases (b) as prices fall, quantity demanded increases (c) as prices rise, demand decreases (d) as prices fall, demand increases **LO 1-1**   17._____

18. If the law of demand is valid, which of the following is true? (a) more people decide to drink coffee, so the demand for coffee increases (b) the quantity demanded of hamburger increases, so the price of hamburger falls (c) the price of iPhones falls, so the quantity demanded of iPhones increases (d) your income increases, so you'll buy more DVDs **LO 1-1**   18._____

19. The sum of all individual demand curves results in a(n) (a) societal demand curve (b) market demand curve (c) absolute demand curve (d) aggregate demand curve **LO 1-2**   19._____

20. How does a market demand curve differ from an individual demand curve? (a) it assumes that all variables are changing constantly (b) it is valid for goods but not for services (c) the relationship between price and quantity demanded is positive, not direct (d) none of these **LO 1-2**   20._____

Part 3 Short Answer

Directions: Read the following questions, and write your response.

21. Logan's demand schedule for milkshakes is shown below. At a price of $2.50, Logan's quantity demanded is two per month. Following the law of demand, what will happen to Logan's quantity demanded as the price falls from $2.50 to $1.00? **LO 1-1**

Point	Price per milkshake	Quantity demanded per month
A	$2.50	2
B	$2.00	?
C	$1.50	?
D	$1.00	?

22. How is a market demand curve created? **LO 1-2**

Part 4 Critical Thinking

Directions: Read the following question, and write your response.

23. Describe an instance in your own life when the law of demand influenced a buying decision. **LO 1-1**

3-2 Shifts in the Demand Curve

Part 1 True or False

Directions: Place a *T* for True or an *F* for False in the Answers column to show whether each of the following statements is true or false.

Answers

1. Price is the only variable that determines how much of a good consumers buy. **LO 2-1**   1._____

2. A change in demand is an increase or decrease in the demand curve. **LO 2-1**   2._____

3. A rightward shift in the demand curve indicates an increase in demand. **LO 2-1**   3._____

4. A price increase has the effect of downward movement along the demand curve. **LO 2-1**   4._____

5. Population growth shifts a market demand curve rightward. **LO 2-2**   5._____

6. When people tire of a product, the demand curve for that product shifts leftward. **LO 2-2**   6._____

7. A used car is an example of a *normal good*. **LO 2-2**   7._____

8. Suppose an unexpected freeze in Florida damages the orange crop. The likely result of this will be for the change in quantity demanded for orange juice will increase. **LO 2-2**   8._____

9. Margarine would be considered a *substitute good* for butter. **LO 2-2**   9._____

10. Complementary goods have an inverse relationship to changes in the demand curve. **LO 2-2**   10._____

Part 2 Multiple Choice

Directions: In the Answers column, write the letter that represents the word, or group of words, that correctly completes the statement or answers the question.

Answers

11. A change in quantity demanded results solely from a change in _____. (a) consumer income (b) consumer taste (c) price (d) number of buyers **LO 2-1**   11._____

12. Which of the following factors can influence the position of the demand curve? (a) consumer expectations (b) prices of related goods (c) consumer income (d) all of these **LO 2-1**   12._____

13. A leftward or rightward shift in the demand curve is called a _____. (a) change in demand (b) change in quantity demanded (c) change in supply (d) change in supply provided **LO 2-1**   13._____

14. A demand shifter factor can cause a(n) _____. (a) decrease in the quantity demanded (b) increase in the quantity demanded (c) decrease or increase in demand (d) all of these **LO 2-1**   14._____

15. Which of the following will shift market demand curves leftward? (a) a once-popular product falls out of favor (b) a population decline (c) price of a substitute good increases (d) all of these **LO 2-2**   15._____

16. A normal good is any good _____. (a) that people buy on a daily basis without much thought (b) for which there is an inverse relationship between changes in income and its demand curve (c) that consumers purchase together with another good (d) for which there is a direct relationship between changes in income and its demand curve **LO 2-2**   16._____

17. All of the following will shift the demand curve for automobiles to the right *except* (a) the   17._____
    local factory gives a big raise to employees (b) a brand new auto dealership opens in town
    (c) the price of gasoline falls (d) none of these **LO 2-2**

18. Which of the following will shift the demand curve rightward for Pepsi? (a) a decrease in the   18._____
    price of Pepsi (b) an increase in the price of Coca-Cola, which is a substitute for Pepsi
    (c) an increase in the price of Pepsi (d) a decrease in the number of Pepsi buyers **LO 2-2**

19. If income increases and the demand for public transportation decreases, what does that tell   19._____
    us? (a) public transportation is a normal good (b) buyers are not acting in their best interests
    (c) public transportation is an inferior good (d) public transportation must be a complement
    with some other good **LO 2-2**

20. Suppose domestic cars and foreign cars are substitutes. If the price of foreign cars falls,   20._____
    the demand curve for domestic cars will _____ (a) shift leftward (b) shift rightward
    (c) shift upward (d) none of these; the change in the price of foreign cars will affect the
    supply curve only, not the demand curve **LO 2-2**

Part 3 Short Answer

Directions: Read the following questions, and write your response.

21. Explain the difference between a change in quantity demanded and a change in demand. **LO 2-1**

22. Name the five non-price determinants. **LO 2-2**

Part 4 Critical Thinking

Directions: Read the following questions, and write your response.

23. What does the following demand curve tell us about the quantity of DVDs being purchased? Which of
    the factors listed below could have caused demand curve D_1 to shift leftward to D_3? **LO 2-2**

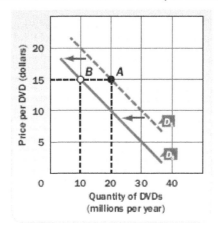

a. a decrease in the price of DVDs

b. an increase in the price of DVD players, a complement to DVDs

c. an increase in the price of Internet movie downloads, a substitute for DVDs

3-3 Elasticity of Demand

Part 1 True or False

Directions: Place a *T* for True or an *F* for False in the Answers column to show whether each of the following statements is true or false.

Answers

1. Total revenue is the total dollars a firm receives from the sale of a good or service. **LO 3-1**
   1. _____

2. Elasticity of demand explains how strongly consumers react to a change in price. **LO 3-1**
   2. _____

3. Inelastic demand exists when the percentage change in quantity demanded is greater than the percentage change in price. **LO 3-1**
   3. _____

4. Demand is elastic when the elasticity value is less than 1. **LO 3-1**
   4. _____

5. Most demand curves have a range where demand is elastic at relatively high prices. **LO 3-1**
   5. _____

6. The price of coffee falls by 5% and the quantity demanded increases by 5%. This is an example of unitary elastic demand. **LO 3-1**
   6. _____

7. Unitary demand is the dividing point between elastic and inelastic demand. **LO 3-1**
   7. _____

8. Businesses need to know about elasticity of demand because it determines the size of total revenue. **LO 3-2**
   8. _____

9. In the inelastic range of a demand curve, as price decreases total revenue increases. **LO 3**
   9. _____

10. Increases in prices do not always result in increases in total revenue. **LO 3-2**
    10. _____

Part 2 Multiple Choice

Directions: In the Answers column, write the letter that represents the word, or group of words, that correctly completes the statement or answers the question.

Answers

11. Price × Quantity demanded = _____. (a) net revenue (b) total profit (c) total revenue (d) net profit **LO 3-1**
    11. _____

12. How do you determine the price elasticity of demand? (a) multiply price times quantity demanded (b) compare the change in quantity supplied to the change in price (c) compare percentage change in quantity demanded to the percentage change in price (d) divide quantity supplied by price **LO 3-1**
    12. _____

13. Suppose the price of ice cream cones increases by 10% and the quantity of ice cream cones demanded falls by 12%. This indicates that demand for ice cream cones is (a) elastic (b) inelastic (c) unitary elastic (d) static **LO 3-1**
    13. _____

14. If the demand for milk is *completely* inelastic, then a 10% increase in milk prices would result in _____. (a) a 10% decrease in the quantity demanded (b) a 10% increase in the quantity demanded (c) no change in the quantity of milk demanded (d) a decrease in total revenue from milk sales **LO 3-1**
    14. _____

15. If the elasticity value for a good is 3, then a 10% increase in the price of that good _____ quantity demanded by _____ percent. (a) increases; 30 (b) decreases; 30 (c) decreases; 3 (d) increases; 7 **LO 3-1**
    15. _____

16. For most demand curves, demand is _____ at relatively high prices. (a) inelastic (b) static (c) unitary (d) elastic **LO 3-1**   16. ____

17. If demand is elastic, the percentage change in quantity demanded is _____ the percentage change in price. (a) greater than (b) less than (c) equal to (d) unrelated to **LO 3-1**   17. ____

18. If a coffee shop raises the price of an espresso drink by 5% and the quantity demanded decreases by 5%, then the demand for espresso is _____ and the coffee shop's total revenue _____. (a) unitary elastic; does not change (b) unitary elastic; increases (c) inelastic; decreases (d) elastic; increases **LO 3-1/LO 3-2**   18. ____

19. Total revenue is at its highest when demand is _____. (a) unitary elastic (b) completely elastic (c) completely inelastic (d) static **LO 3-2**   19. ____

20. Suppose the price of a good is $30 and demand is elastic. In this case, a price _____ would _____ total revenue (a) cut; decrease (b) increase; increase (c) cut; increase (d) increase; have no effect on **LO 3-2**   20. ____

Part 3 Short Answer

Directions: Read the following questions, and write your response.

21. Do you think the demand for gold jewelry is elastic, inelastic, or unitary elastic? Explain your answer. **LO 3-1**

22. Suppose the elasticity value for a product is 0.65. Is demand elastic or inelastic? How responsive would quantity demanded be to a change in price? **LO 3-1**

23. Why does a business need to know whether demand for its goods is elastic or inelastic at different prices? **LO 3-2**

Part 4 Critical Thinking

Directions: Read the following questions, and write your response.

24. Name two products or services for which you have elastic demand and two products or services for which you have inelastic demand. Explain your answers. **LO 3-1**

25. Products that are highly elastic in demand often have many substitutes. Why do you think this is true? **LO 3-1**

Chapter 3 Market Demand

Chapter 3 Review

Part 1 True or False

Directions: Place a *T* for True or an *F* for False in the Answers column to show whether each of the following statements is true or false.

Answers

1. Demand is the amount of goods and services purchased at a given price. **LO 1-1**   1._____

2. The demand schedule is formed by the line connecting points that represent possible   2._____
    combinations of price and quantity purchased by consumers. **LO 1-1**

3. A market demand curve is the sum of all individual demand curves. **LO 1-2**   3._____

4. A change in quantity demanded is based on the assumption that all demand shifter factors   4._____
    remain constant; only price changes. **LO 2-1**

5. The demand curve shifts only if all five demand shifter factors change. **LO 2-1**   5._____

6. An *inferior good* is a good that is in low demand. **LO 2-2**   6._____

7. There is an inverse relationship between a price change for one good and the demand for its   7._____
    substitute good. **LO 2-2**

8. *Elasticity of demand* shows consumer responsiveness to a change in price. **LO 3-1**   8._____

9. A product has an elasticity of demand value of 0.55, indicating that demand is elastic.   9._____
    LO 3-1

10. Knowledge of elasticity of demand helps businesses make pricing decisions that result in the   10._____
    greatest total revenue. **LO 3-2**

Part 2 Multiple Choice

Directions: In the Answers column, write the letter that represents the word, or group of words, that correctly completes the statement or answers the question.

Answers

11. The demand curve is downward sloping because _____. (a) there is a direct relationship   11._____
    between price and quantity demanded (b) as costs increase, so does price (c) as price
    decreases, quantity demanded increases (d) increased prices equals increased revenue **LO 1-1**

12. A demand curve shows how many hamburgers Martin will purchase at a given price.   12._____
    This is an example of a(n) _____ demand curve. (a) aggregate (b) individual (c) market
    (d) synthetic **LO 1-2**

13. Which of the following is *not* considered a demand shifter? (a) number of buyers (b) price   13._____
    (c) expectations (d) consumer income **LO 2-1**

14. A price decrease causes _____. (a) a decrease in the quantity demanded (b) rightward   14._____
    shift in the demand curve (c) downward movement along the demand curve (d) leftward shift
    in the demand curve **LO 2-1**

15. The population of a country increased by 10% over the past decade. What is the likely effect   15._____
    on the market demand curve for bread? (a) there has been no change as bread is a highly
    elastic good (b) the demand curve shifted leftward (c) the slope of the demand curve changed
    by 10 degrees (d) the demand curve shifted rightward **LO 2-2**

16. As buyers receive higher incomes, the demand curve for steak shifts rightward. This indicates that steak is a _____. (a) substitute good for hamburger (b) complementary good to wine (c) normal good (d) inferior good **LO 2-2**   16. _____

17. Which of the following is *most likely* a complementary good to golf clubs? (a) golf balls (b) tennis rackets (c) luxury automobiles (d) all of these **LO 2-2**   17. _____

18. The price elasticity of demand is the ratio of the _____ to the _____. (a) change in quantity demanded; change in price (b) percentage change in quantity demanded; percentage change in price (c) change in price; change in quantity demanded (d) percentage change in price; percentage change in quantity demanded **LO 3-1**   18. _____

19. Demand is inelastic if the elasticity of demand value is _____. (a) positive (b) negative (c) greater than 1 (d) less than 1 **LO 3-1**   19. _____

20. The elasticity of demand for luxury cars is likely to be _____. (a) smaller than the elasticity of demand for bread (b) larger than the elasticity of demand for bread (c) unitary elastic (d) less than 1 **LO 3-1**   20. _____

Part 3 Short Answer

Directions: Read the following question, and write your response.

21. Complete the table to summarize the effects of changes in price and demand shifter factors on the demand curve. **LO 2-1**

Change	Effect	Description
Price increases		
	Downward movement along the demand curve	
		Decrease or increase in demand

Part 4 Critical Thinking

Directions: Read the following question, and write your response.

22. Relate each of the five demand shifter factors to demand for butter. **LO 2-2**

4-1 The Law of Supply

Part 1 True or False

Directions: Place a *T* for True or an *F* for False in the Answers column to show whether each of the following statements is true or false.

Answers

1. When economists refer to *supply*, they mean a specific quantity of an item on sale. **LO 1-1**   1._____

2. *Quantity supplied* is the amount of goods or services sellers offer for sale at a given price. **LO 1-1**   2._____

3. In a free enterprise system, sellers have a profit incentive to charge higher prices. **LO 1-1**   3._____

4. If price goes up, suppliers will devote more resources to a product. **LO 1-1**   4._____

5. The demand schedule lists the quantity of a good or service a business offers for sale at possible prices. **LO 1-1**   5._____

6. The supply curve is a summary of a consumer's buying intentions. **LO 1-1**   6._____

7. The supply curve shows that higher prices encourage production. **LO 1-1**   7._____

8. Individual supply curves vary from producer to producer. **LO 1-2**   8._____

9. The law of supply applies both to individuals and to entire markets. **LO 1-2**   9._____

10. Unlike the market demand curve, the assumption for the market supply curve is that all variables are constantly changing. **LO 1-2**   10._____

Part 2 Multiple Choice

Directions: In the Answers column, write the letter that represents the word, or group of words, that correctly completes the statement or answers the question.

Answers

11. Which of the following statements is incorrect? (a) *Supply* is the relationship between the price and quantity supplied for a good or service. (b) Supply is based on the assumption that other variables remain unchanged. (c) To economists, the terms *quantity* and *quantity supplied* have the same meaning. (d) All of these statements are incorrect. **LO 1-1**   11._____

12. The law of supply states that as price decreases _____. (a) demand decreases (b) quantity demanded decreases (c) quantity supplied increases (d) quantity supplied decreases **LO 1-1**   12._____

13. The quantity supplied of a good is _____. (a) equal to the difference between quantity available and quantity demanded (b) the amount a producer would sell if it had unlimited resources (c) the amount producers are willing to supply at a given price (d) the same thing as quantity demanded at each price **LO 1-1**   13._____

14. Falling prices cause a textile company to reduce the quantity of fabric it is willing to produce. This illustrates _____. (a) the law of supply (b) the law of demand (c) that its fabrics are inferior goods (d) that its fabrics are substitute goods **LO 1-1**   14._____

15. As the price of a good rises, there is greater _____. (a) demand (b) profit (c) consumer interest (d) all of these **LO 1-1**   15._____

16. If prices increase, producers become _____. (a) more willing and more able to supply goods (b) less willing and less able to supply goods (c) more willing but less able to supply goods (d) less willing but more able to supply goods **LO 1-1**   16._____

17. A supply schedule for tablet computers would show _____. (a) the profits sellers have
made on tablets (b) the quantity of tablets consumers demand at various prices (c) the quantity
of tablets sellers have already sold (d) the quantity of tablets sellers offer for sale at possible
prices **LO 1-1**

17._____

18. Which statement about supply curves is *correct*? (a) supply curves assume that all other
variables are held constant (b) the supply curve is formed by connecting points that represent
possible combinations of price and quantity purchased by consumers (c) the supply curve can
tell you how many items a buyer will purchase (d) a supply curve can be formed for tangible
goods but not for services **LO 1-1**

18._____

19. The market supply curve shows _____. (a) the total quantity demanded by all consumers
at various prices (b) the total quantity supplied by all producers at various prices (c) neither a
nor b (d) both a and b **LO 1-2**

19._____

20. Suppose you want to understand how increasing the price of electric guitars is affecting the
electric guitar supply. Which of the following would you examine? (a) the aggregate supply
curve (b) the individual supply curve (c) the market supply curve (d) none of these **LO 1-2**

20._____

Part 3 Short Answer

Directions: Read the following questions, and write your response.

21. Why are sellers willing to sell more at a higher price? **LO 1-1**

22. How is a market supply curve created? **LO 1-2**

23. Why is the supply curve upward sloping? Is the relationship between price and quantity supplied direct or
inverse? **LO 1-1**

24. How is a market supply curve created? **LO 1-2**

Part 4 Critical Thinking

25. Create a supply schedule using the information provided in the supply curve. **LO 1-1**

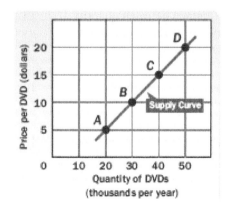
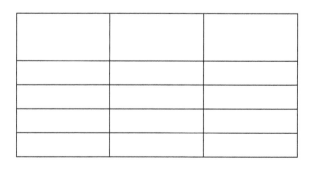

Chapter 4 Market Supply and Price Determination

4-2 Shifts in the Supply Curve

Part 1 True or False

Directions: Place a *T* for True or an *F* for False in the Answers column to show whether each of the following statements is true or false.

Answers

1. A change in quantity supplied can result from an increase in the number of sellers. **LO 2-1**

    1._____

2. A *change in supply* is not the same as a *change in quantity supplied*. **LO 2-1**

    2._____

3. A leftward shift in the supply curve indicates an increase in supply. **LO 2-1**

    3._____

4. The price of french fries at Burger King decreases. This should result in a decrease in the quantity supplied. **LO 2-1**

    4._____

5. The price of a product is the only factor that influences how much sellers offer for sale. **LO 2-2**

    5._____

6. If more ice cream shops enter a market, the supply curve for ice cream will move rightward **LO 2-2**

    6._____

7. An increase in the price of labor adds to the cost of production. **LO 2-2**

    7._____

8. An excise tax affects supply similarly to an increase in resource price. **LO 2-2**

    8._____

9. Producer expectations affect current supply but not current demand. **LO 2-2**

    9._____

10. The number of sellers has a direct relationship with changes in the supply curve. **LO 2-2**

    10._____

Part 2 Multiple Choice

Directions: In the Answers column, write the letter that represents the word, or group of words, that correctly completes the statement or answers the question.

Answers

11. If the price of a product changes but all other factors remain constant, the result will be _____. (a) a new supply curve (b) movement along the demand curve (c) movement along the supply curve (d) a rightward or leftward shift in the demand curve **LO 2-1**

    11._____

12. A decrease in quantity supplied will result in a _____. (a) leftward shift in the supply curve (b) rightward shift in the supply curve (c) movement up the supply curve (d) movement down the supply curve **LO 2-1**

    12._____

13. Which of the following results solely from a change in price? (a) change in quantity supplied (b) change in supply (c) change in demand (d) all of these **LO 2-1**

    13._____

14. A supply shifter factor can cause a(n) _____. (a) decrease in the quantity supplied (b) increase in the quantity supplied (c) decrease or increase in supply (d) all of these **LO 2-1**

    14._____

15. A rightward shift in the supply curve indicates a(n) _____. (a) decrease in supply (b) increase in supply (c) decrease in quantity supplied (d) increase in quantity supplied **LO 2-1**

    15._____

16. Which of the following is *not* a supply shifter factor? (a) number of consumers (b) technology (c) resource prices (d) taxes and subsidies **LO 2-2**

    16._____

17. Which of the following would not shift the supply curve? (a) an increase in the price of the good (b) an increase in the wages of employees (c) entry of new producers into the market (d) lowering trade barriers on imports **LO 2-2**

    17._____

18. The supply curve for scooters will shift leftward if _____. (a) quantity demanded exceeds   18._____
quantity supplied (b) there is an increase in the cost of machinery used to produce scooters
(c) better technology makes it easier to produce scooters (d) taxes levied on the scooter factory
go down **LO 2-2**

19. A tax paid by the seller on the production or sale of a good or service is called a(n) _____.   19._____
(a) value-added tax (b) tariff (c) subsidy (d) excise tax **LO 2-2**

20. Suppose the price of corn rises but the price of wheat remains the same. Which of the   20._____
following scenarios is *most likely*? (a) increase in supply of corn and decrease in supply of
wheat (b) decrease in supply of corn and increase in supply of wheat (c) increase in supply of
both corn and wheat (d) decrease in supply of both corn and wheat **LO 2-2**

Part 3 Short Answer

Directions: Read the following questions, and write your response.

21. Fill in the blanks in the following statements to make them correct. **LO 2-1**

A change in _____ is caused by a change in _____, and is represented by movement along
the supply curve.

A change in _____ is caused by a change in_____, and is represented by a
rightward or leftward shift in the supply curve.

22. Name the six supply shifter factors. **LO 2-2**

Part 4 Critical Thinking

23. a. In the supply curve shown below, the development of a more efficient technology for drilling oil could
cause movement from point _____ to point _____.

b. A decrease in the quantity of oil supplied but *not* in the supply is shown by a movement from point
_____ to point _____. **LO 2-1/LO 2-2**

Chapter 4 Market Supply and Price Determination

4-3 The Free Market Price

Part 1 True or False

Directions: Place a *T* for True or an *F* for False in the Answers column to show whether each of the following statements is true or false.

Answers

1. A surplus occurs at any price at which the quantity supplied is greater than the quantity demanded. **LO 3-1**

   1._____

2. When a product is in short supply, there is downward pressure on price. **LO 3-1**

   2._____

3. In the case of excess demand, unsatisfied consumers compete to obtain the product by bidding to pay a higher price. **LO 3-1**

   3._____

4. Disequilibrium is a temporary condition. **LO 3-1**

   4._____

5. In the free enterprise system, price plays a rationing role. **LO 3-1**

   5._____

6. Prices are set by sellers adding a certain percentage to their costs; if sellers' costs rise, they simply raise these prices by that percentage. **LO 3-2**

   6._____

7. Demand for product X increases, causing the demand curve to shift rightward. This will lead to a decrease in the equilibrium price. **LO 3-2**

   7._____

8. Demand for product X increases, causing the demand curve to shift rightward. This will lead to a temporary shortage of product X. **LO 3-2**

   8._____

9. An increase in supply will lead to a decrease in the equilibrium price. **LO 3-2**

   9._____

10. Suppose a hard freeze kills much of the Florida orange crop. This will ultimately lead to an increase in the equilibrium price for orange juice and a decrease in the quantity of orange juice demanded by consumers. **LO 3-2**

    10._____

Part 2 Multiple Choice

Directions: In the Answers column, write the letter that represents the word, or group of words, that correctly completes the statement or answers the question.

Answers

11. Because of a warm winter, Sam's Hardware has an excess supply of snow shovels in stock. Sam will *most likely* _____. (a) raise the price of snow shovels (b) never carry snow shovels in his store again (c) offer a discount on snow shovels (d) go out of business **LO 3-1**

    11._____

12. There will be a surplus of cheese when _____. (a) price is below the equilibrium level (b) the supply curve slopes downward and the demand curve slopes upward (c) the demand and supply curves do not intersect (d) consumers want to buy less than producers offer for sale **LO 3-1**

    12._____

13. This occurs at any price at which the quantity supplied is less than the quantity demanded. (a) surplus (b) shortage (c) equilibrium (d) panic buying **LO 3-1**

    13._____

14. The price of carpet falls if _____. (a) quantity demanded exceeds quantity supplied (b) the current price is below equilibrium (c) there is a surplus at the current price (d) all of these **LO 3-1**

    14._____

15. Which of the following statements is *incorrect*? (a) Disequilibrium occurs at a market price at which quantity demanded does not equal quantity supplied. (b) Disequilibrium can become a permanent condition in a bad economy. (c) Trial-and-error makes all possible price-quantity combinations unstable except at equilibrium. (d) all of these **LO 3-1**

    15._____

16. All other factors remaining constant, there is no incentive for buyers or sellers to change their decisions when _____. (a) disequilibrium occurs (b) there is excess demand (c) there is a surplus of goods (d) prices are at equilibrium **LO 3-1**   16._____

17. Which of the following will cause a shortage of corn? (a) demand for corn decreases (b) supply of corn decreases (c) supply of corn increases (d) all of these **LO 3-2**   17._____

18. Under which conditions will equilibrium price *increase*? (a) decreased demand, increased supply (b) decreased demand, no change in supply (c) increased demand, decreased supply (d) increased supply, no change in demand **LO 3-2**   18._____

19. Which of the following causation chains is accurate? (a) increase in demand → increase in equilibrium price → increase in quantity supplied (b) decrease in demand → increase in equilibrium price → decrease in quantity supplied (c) both of these (d) neither of these **LO 3-2**   19._____

20. Supply decrease will _____ the equilibrium price and _____ equilibrium quantity. (a) increase; decrease (b) decrease; increase (c) decrease; decrease (d) increase; increase **LO 3-2**   20._____

Part 3 Short Answer

Directions: Read the following questions, and write your response.

21. Briefly explain how price adjustment eliminates a shortage. **LO 3-1**

22. The following table describes the gasoline market in Lexington, Kentucky. Suppose the price of a gallon of gasoline is $3.68. Is there a surplus, a shortage, or is the market in equilibrium? **LO 3-1**

Price per gallon	Quantity demanded (in gallons)	Quantity supplied (in gallons)
$3.73	340,000	420,000
$3.68	360,000	405,000
$3.65	370,000	370,000
$3.62	375,000	355,000

23. What will happen to the equilibrium price of iPhones if demand increases and supply decreases? **LO 3-2**

Part 4 Critical Thinking

Directions: Read the following questions, and write your response.

24. Explain why prices above or below the equilibrium level are not stable in the long run. **LO 3-1**

25. How would increased incomes affect the equilibrium price and quantity demanded of bus rides? Explain. **LO 3-2**

4-4 Role of Government in Free Enterprise

Part 1 True or False

Directions: Place a *T* for True or an *F* for False in the Answers column to show whether each of the following statements is true or false.

Answers

1. Price ceilings are illegal in the United States. **LO 4-1**

   1._____

2. Rent controls result in a shortage of rental units. **LO 4-1**

   2._____

3. If the government imposed a ceiling on the price of gasoline, one likely result would be long lines at the gas pumps. **LO 4-1**

   3._____

4. The legally established lowest wage rate that can be paid to workers is called a *living wage*. **LO 4-1**

   4._____

5. There is a direct relationship between the quantity of unskilled labor employers are willing to hire and the wage rate. **LO 4-1**

   5._____

6. In *The Wealth of Nations*, Adam Smith strongly advocated against all government regulation of the free enterprise system. **LO 4-2**

   6._____

7. Regulations are government rules or laws designed to control business. **LO 4-2**

   7._____

8. In the United States, the trend since the 1980s has been toward increased government restrictions on businesses and industries. **LO 4-2**

   8._____

9. The Interstate Commerce Commission was established in 1887 to regulate rail prices and cut the cost of rail transportation. **LO 4-2**

   9._____

10. An important deregulation case involved the dismantling of AT&T. **LO 4-2**

    10._____

Part 2 Multiple Choice

Directions: In the Answers column, write the letter that represents the word, or group of words, that correctly completes the statement or answers the question.

Answers

11. Rent control is an example of a(n) _____. (a) price floor (b) tariff (c) price ceiling (d) property tax **LO 4-1**

    11._____

12. What is the effect of rent controls on consumers? (a) consumers spend less time searching for rental units (b) some will be tempted to sublet rental units to the highest bidder (c) eviction rates will rise (d) all of these **LO 4-1**

    12._____

13. What would happen if a price ceiling on milk is set *above* the equilibrium price? (a) there would be a shortage of milk (b) there would be a surplus of milk (c) there would be neither a surplus nor a shortage of milk (d) milk producers would begin to go out of business **LO 4-1**

    13._____

14. If the minimum wage is raised to $10/hour, a likely result is _____. (a) businesses will hire fewer workers (b) the number of workers willing to offer their labor moves down along the supply curve (c) there will be a shortage of labor (d) all of these **LO 4-1**

    14._____

15. The equilibrium price for a gallon of gasoline is $5/gallon. If the government imposes a price floor of $4/gallon, _____. (a) supply of gasoline increases (b) demand for gasoline decreases (c) the quantity supplied of gasoline will fall short of the quantity demanded (d) the quantity supplied of gasoline will exceed the quantity demanded **LO 4-1**

    15._____

16. Which American industry faced extensive regulation in the late nineteenth century? (a) coal   16. _____
mining (b) farming (c) railroads (d) telecommunications **LO 4-2**

17. This agency was established to protect the public against injury from unsafe products.   17. _____
(a) Consumer Product Safety Commission (b) Occupational Safety and Health
Administration (c) Environmental Protection Agency (d) Federal Communications
Commission **LO 4-2**

18. Which of the following statements about deregulation is *correct*? (a) deregulation has   18. _____
resulted in sharply higher prices in affected industries (b) deregulation reached its peak in the
1970s (c) transportation industries have largely been unaffected by deregulation (d) higher
production costs resulting from regulation has spurred the deregulation trend **LO 4-2**

19. This government agency regulates television and radio broadcasts. (a) Department of   19. _____
Homeland Security (b) Federal Communications Commission (c) Securities and Exchange
Commission (d) Federal Trade Commission **LO 4-2**

20. Which of the following scenarios would the Food and Drug Administration most likely   20. _____
investigate? (a) a self-proclaimed millionaire offers to sell his "get rich secrets" via an
infomercial broadcast on cable TV (b) a pharmaceutical company claims the use of its
products can help you lose 10 pounds in just one week (c) local residents report a foul odor
coming from a nearby chemical factory (d) malfunctioning electric blankets cause fires in at
least a dozen homes **LO 4-2**

Part 3 Short Answer

Directions: Read the following questions, and write your response.

21. From the seller's perspective, rent controls encourage two undesirable effects. What are they? **LO 4-1**

22. Successful deregulation of an industry would be expected to provide what two results? **LO 4-2**

Part 4 Critical Thinking

Directions: Read the following questions, and write your response.

23. Suppose the government imposes price controls on ticket prices for Major League baseball games. Give
one possible advantage and disadvantage consumers would experience as a result. **LO 4-1**

24. The demand and supply schedules for deluxe hamburgers are shown below. What would be the result of a
price ceiling of $2 per burger? **LO 4-2**

Price per burger	Quantity supplied per week	Quantity demanded per week
$1	10	50
$2	20	40
$3	30	30
$4	40	20

Chapter 4 Review

Part 1 True or False

Directions: Place a *T* for True or an *F* for False in the Answers column to show whether each of the following statements is true or false.

Answers

1. Supply is based on the assumption that other variables remain unchanged. **LO 1-1**   1. _____

2. An individual supply curve is the supply for a single seller. **LO 1-2**   2. _____

3. A price increase results in a decrease of the quantity supplied. **LO 2-1**   3. _____

4. The impact of a tax increase on the supply curve is similar to a rise in the cost of labor or any other productive resource. **LO 2-2**   4. _____

5. Equilibrium price is reached when quantity supplied is equal to quantity demanded. **LO 3-1**   5. _____

6. Once an equilibrium price is established, it will never change. **LO 3-2**   6. _____

7. One can reasonably predict that a major forest fire will ultimately lead to a decrease in the equilibrium price of lumber. **LO 3-2**   7. _____

8. An illegal market, or black market, can arise because of the shortage of rental units created by rent controls. **LO 4-1**   8. _____

9. Loss of minimum wage jobs represents a loss of entry-level jobs to those who seek to enter the workforce. **LO 4-1**   9. _____

10. Though government regulation was widespread in the early twentieth century, it rarely affects American businesses or consumers today. **LO 4-2**   10. _____

Part 2 Multiple Choice

Directions: In the Answers column, write the letter that represents the word, or group of words, that correctly completes the statement or answers the question.

Answers

11. The law of supply says that there is a(n) _____ relationship between the price of a good and the quantity sellers offer for sale. (a) direct (b) inverse (c) negative (d) neutral **LO 1-1**   11. _____

12. Which of the following does *not* result from a change in price? (a) change in quantity demanded (b) change in quantity supplied (c) change in supply (d) movement between points along a stationary supply curve **LO 2-1**   12. _____

13. An increase in quantity supplied will result in a _____. (a) leftward shift in the supply curve (b) rightward shift in the supply curve (c) movement up the supply curve (d) movement down the supply curve **LO 2-1**   13. _____

14. Application of better technology in the automotive industry will result in a _____. (a) leftward shift in the supply curve (b) rightward shift in the supply curve (c) movement up the supply curve (d) movement down the supply curve **LO 2-2**   14. _____

15. What happens to the price of a good when there is a shortage of that good? (a) price decreases (b) equilibrium is achieved (c) price is not affected (d) price increases **LO 3-1**   15. _____

16. Which of the following will lead to an increase in quantity supplied? (a) increase in demand (b) decrease in demand (c) decrease in supply (d) all of these **LO 3-2**   16. _____

17. Suppose a firm supplies 1 million boxes of organic corn flakes, but consumers demand 2 million boxes. In this case, _____. (a) there is a surplus of corn flakes (b) the price of organic corn flakes will decrease (c) there is a shortage of corn flakes (d) the market has reached equilibrium **LO 3-1**

17. _____

18. A minimum wage is an example of _____. (a) the "invisible hand" (b) a price floor (c) a price ceiling (d) equilibrium pricing **LO 4-1**

18. _____

19. The removal of government restrictions or controls on a market is called _____. (a) disequilibrium (b) deregulation (c) dysfunction (d) delimitation **LO 4-2**

19. _____

20. What does the Federal Trade Commission do? (a) enforces rules involving safety and health issues in the workplace (b) provides for complete financial disclosure and protects investors (c) enforces antitrust laws and monitors unfair business practices (d) regulates rail prices and outlaws price discrimination **LO 4-2**

20. _____

Part 3 Short Answer

Directions: Read the following questions, and write your response.

21. What is a supply schedule? **LO 1-1**

22. What is a subsidy? What effect do subsidies have on the supply curve? **LO 2-2**

23. The equilibrium price for Justin Bieber T-shirts is $20 and the equilibrium quantity is 5,000. At $15, would there be a shortage or surplus? What kind of pressure would be placed on price, upward or downward? What about at $25 per shirt? **LO 3-1**

Part 4 Critical Thinking

Directions: Read the following question, and write your response.

24. The Environmental Protection Agency is considering new, more stringent clean air regulations on U.S. industry. These regulations would likely be very costly to businesses. In the space below, explain some of the advantages of such regulations. Then list some disadvantages. **LO 4-2**

5-1 Pure Competition and Monopoly

Part 1 True or False

Directions: Place a *T* for True or an *F* for False in the Answers column to show whether each of the following statements is true or false.

Answers

1. All firms sell goods and services under the same market conditions. **LO 1-1**   1._____

2. One characteristic of a purely competitive market is a small number of large firms. **LO 1-1**   2._____

3. No real-world market exactly fits all the assumptions of pure competition. **LO 1-1**   3._____

4. A firm in pure competition can set whatever prices it chooses on its products. **LO 1-1**   4._____

5. Under a monopoly, the consumer must either buy the monopolist's product by paying the asking price or do without it. **LO 1-2**   5._____

6. Because it has a unique product, the monopolist faces little or no competition. **LO 1-2**   6._____

7. In a monopoly, there are no barriers to prevent new firms from entering a market. **LO 1-2**   7._____

8. Patents and copyrights are a form of government barriers to entry into a market. **LO 1-2**   8._____

9. Consumers never benefit from cost savings in a natural monopoly. **LO 1-2**   9._____

10. A *price taker* is a seller that does not consider competition when setting its price. **LO 1-2**   10._____

Part 2 Multiple Choice

Directions: In the Answers column, write the letter that represents the word, or group of words, that correctly completes the statement or answers the question.

Answers

11. A market structure describes the key characteristics of a market, which include (a) the number of firms (b) the similarity of the products sold (c) ease of entry into market (d) all of these.   11._____

12. Pure competition is characterized by all of the following *except* _____. (a) identical products (b) relentless and widespread advertising (c) a large number of buyers and sellers (d) easy entry into or exit from the market **LO 1-1**   12._____

13. A barrier to entry is _____. (a) a government regulation that prohibits a monopoly from existing in a market (b) easy for firms to overcome in monopolistic markets (c) anything that protects a business from competing firms entering a market (d) illegal in most markets **LO 1-1**   13._____

14. Which of the following is the best example of a purely competitive market? (a) diamonds (b) fast food (c) farming (d) airline industry **LO 1-1**   14._____

15. When a business is a *price taker*, it _____. (a) sells at the price recommended by its suppliers (b) bases its selling price on recommendations from the government (c) can set whatever price it wants on its products (d) has no control over the selling price of its product **LO 1-1**   15._____

16. Which of these is *not* a characteristic of a monopoly? (a) single seller (b) unique product (c) price taker (d) impossible entry **LO 1-2**   16._____

17. Which of the following is the best example of a monopoly? (a) the only drugstore in a remote rural town (b) a McDonald's restaurant located in the heart of Manhattan (c) the publisher of your economics textbook (d) all of these are monopolies **LO 1-2**   17._____

18. The purpose of patents and copyrights is to _____. (a) stimulate economic competition (b) encourage innovation and new products (c) make it easier for businesses to enter markets (d) allow firms to become price takers **LO 1-2**   18._____

19. Which of the following is *not* an example of a barrier to entry? (a) control of a natural resource (b) a copyright (c) size of firm (d) a natural monopoly **LO 1-2**   19._____

A natural monopoly can be created if _____. (a) new technology allows a single firm to produce at a lower average cost than two or more firms (b) a government license is required before the firm can sell the product (c) the firm retains ownership of all necessary resources (d) all of these **LO 1-2**   20._____

Part 3 Short Answer

Directions: Read the following questions, and write your response.

21. What is the effect of having a "large number" of small firms in a purely competitive market? **LO 1-1**

22. Why doesn't a monopolist need to check daily reports to find out the market price of its product? **LO 1-2**

23. Use the graphic organizer to identify the characteristics of pure competition and monopoly. **LO 1-1 &1-2**

Characteristics of Pure Competition	
Characteristics of Monopoly	

Part 4 Critical Thinking

Directions: Read the following question, and write your response.

24. Explain why a purely competitive firm's demand curve would be horizontal. **LO 1-1**

5-2 Monopolistic Competition and Oligopoly

Part 1 True or False

Directions: Place a *T* for True or an *F* for False in the Answers column to show whether each of the following statements is true or false.

Answers

1. A business that operates in a monopolistically competitive market has a degree of power to maximize profit. **LO 2-1** 1._____

2. In monopolistic competition, the number of sellers is greater than in pure competition. **LO 2-1** 2._____

3. Product differentiation can be real or imagined, but it does not matter which is correct as long as consumers believe that differences exist. **LO 2-1** 3._____

4. Monopolistic competition is by far the most common market structure in the United States. **LO 2-1** 4._____

5. Businesses that operate in monopolistically competitive markets have little incentive to advertise because advertising expenses would simply reduce profits. **LO 2-1** 5._____

6. Oligopolies are almost never found in real-world markets. **LO 2-2** 6._____

7. An oligopoly is a market in which an action by one firm generally causes a reaction from other firms. **LO 2-2** 7._____

8. Firms operating in an oligopoly all produce identical products. **LO 2-2** 8._____

9. There are few barriers to entry in an oligopoly. **LO 2-2** 9._____

10. Cartels are illegal in the United States, but not in many other nations. **LO 2-2** 10._____

Part 2 Multiple Choice

Directions: In the Answers column, write the letter that represents the word, or group of words, that correctly completes the statement or answers the question.

Answers

11. The key feature of monopolistic competition is _____. (a) product differentiation (b) size of firms in the market (c) number of firms in the market (d) difficult entry into the market **LO 2-1** 11._____

12. In monopolistic competition, (a) there are only a few large firms (b) firms are price takers (c) businesses face low barriers to entry (d) all of these **LO 2-1** 12._____

13. A differentiated product has _____. (a) close but no perfect substitutes (b) many perfect substitutes (c) no close substitutes (d) no substitutes of any kind **LO 2-1** 13._____

14. Which of the following is different about pure competition and monopolistic competition? (a) there are more sellers in a monopolistically competitive market (b) monopolistically competitive firms have some control over price (c) it is much more difficult to enter a purely competitive market (d) prices in a monopolistically competitive market are identical **LO 2-1** 14._____

15. Taco Bell, Long John Silver's, McDonald's, and Arby's are best described as operating in which of the following market structures? (a) oligopoly (b) monopolistic competition (c) natural monopoly (d) pure competition **LO 2-1** 15._____

16. Which of the following market types has only a few competing businesses? (a) oligopoly   16._____
    (b) monopoly (c) pure competition (d) monopolistic competition **LO 2-2**

17. An oligopoly _____. (a) talks to rival firms to determine the best price for all of them to   17._____
    charge (b) asks the government to set the price of its products (c) has some influence over the
    price of its products (d) none of these **LO 2-2**

18. Which of the following businesses operates in an oligopolistic market? (a) Walgreen's   18._____
    Pharmacy (b) K-Mart (c) the corner barbershop (d) General Motors **LO 2-2**

19. One major difference between oligopoly and monopolistic competition is that _____.   19._____
    (a) businesses in an oligopoly never advertise (b) businesses in an oligopoly do not produce
    differentiated products (c) entry is more difficult in oligopoly (d) there are more firms in an
    oligopoly **LO 2-2**

20. A *cartel* is an organization set up to regulate the _____. (a) demand for a product (b) price 20._____
    and output of a product (c) employees' wages (d) product quality **LO 2-2**

Part 3 Short Answer

Directions: Read the following questions, and write your response.

21. Firms in a monopolistically competitive market are price makers, not price takers. Explain the primary
    reason for this. **LO 2-1**

22. Why is research and development so important to oligopolists? **LO 2-2**

Part 4 Critical Thinking

Directions: Read the following questions, and write your response.

23. In a monopolistically competitive market, what is the desired effect of advertising on the demand curve?
    LO 2-1

24. Why do firms in an oligopolistic market structure watch one another's moves closely? **LO 2-2**

Chapter 5 Review

Part 1 True or False

Directions: Place a *T* for True or an *F* for False in the Answers column to show whether each of the following statements is true or false.

Answers

1. Firms sell goods and services under different market conditions, which economists call *target markets*. **LO 1-1**   1._____

2. It is very difficult to enter a purely competitive market. **LO 1-1**   2._____

3. Pure competition and monopoly are very similar; the major difference is the size of the firms. **LO 1-2**   3._____

4. Sole control of a strategic input is one way a monopolist can prevent a newcomer from entering a market. **LO 1-2**   4._____

5. In monopolistic competition, no single seller has a large enough share of the market to completely control prices. **LO 2-1**   5._____

6. Under monopolistic competition, when one business raises prices all consumers begin buying from a different business. **LO 2-1**   6._____

7. Major oligopolists often compete using advertising to display product differentiation. **LO 2-2**   7._____

8. The U.S. airline industry can be fairly characterized as an oligopoly. **LO 2-2**   8._____

9. The goal of a cartel is to reap monopoly profits by replacing competition with cooperation. **LO 2-2**   9._____

10. The most important characteristic that distinguishes one market structure from another is the size of the firms in the market. **LO 2-2**   10._____

Part 2 Multiple Choice

Directions: In the Answers column, write the letter that represents the word, or group of words, that correctly completes the statement or answers the question.

Answers

11. Which of the following market types has all firms selling products so identical that buyers do not care from which firm they buy? (a) oligopoly (b) natural monopoly (c) pure competition (d) monopolistic competition **LO 1-1**   11._____

12. When the products of all the firms in a market are homogeneous, _____. (a) the firms in the market are all price makers (b) all firms in the market charge the same price (c) some customers would pay a higher price if a firm raised its prices (d) customers ask for a product by its brand name **LO 1-1**   12._____

13. Which of the following market structures has the fewest number of firms? (a) monopolistic competition (b) pure competition (c) monopoly (d) oligopoly **LO 1-2**   13._____

14. Which of the following is the best example of a natural monopoly? (a) natural gas company (b) fast-food company (c) automobile manufacturer (d) farmer **LO 1-2**   14._____

15. If a monopolistically competitive business can convince consumers that its product is of better quality and value than products sold by other businesses in the same market, then _____. (a) demand will become more elastic (b) the business loses control over price (c) demand increases (d) all of these **LO 2-1**
15._____

16. Which of the following firms operates in a monopolistically competitive market? (a) gas stations (b) convenience stores (c) fitness centers (d) all of these **LO 2-1**
16._____

17. Which of the following statements about advertising is incorrect? (a) It reduces product differentiation. (b) It is more important in markets with monopolistic competition than in markets with pure competition. (c) It can reduce consumer sensitivity to price changes. (d) All of these statements are incorrect. **LO 2-1**
17._____

18. Which of these would *not* be considered an example of product differentiation in monopolistic competition? (a) better quality (b) location of the retail store (c) new and improved packaging (d) product price **LO 2-1**
18._____

19. A firm's influence over the price of the good produced in monopoly, oligopoly, monopolistic competition, and pure competition, respectively, is _____. (a) significant, none, slight, total (b) none, slight, significant, total (c) total, significant, slight, none (d) slight, none, total, significant **LO 2-2**
19._____

20. One characteristic of pure competition that distinguishes it from the other three market structures is that _____. (a) there are large and small firms in the industry (b) the firms are all price takers (c) the product is unique (d) there are many barriers to enter the market **LO 2-2**
20._____

Part 3 Short Answer

Directions: Read the following questions, and write your response.

21. Why are purely competitive firms price takers? **LO 1-1**

22. Order the four market structures according to the ease of entry for new firms from easy entry to most difficult entry. **LO 2-2**

23. Why might an oligopolist compete through product differentiation rather than price competition? **LO 1-1, LO 2-2**

Part 4 Critical Thinking

Directions: Read the following question, and write your response.

24. Think about your daily purchases. How are they distributed among the different market structures discussed in this chapter? Give examples of goods and services you purchase or use from each market structure. **LO 1-2**

6-1 Business in America

Part 1 True or False

Directions: Place a *T* for True or an *F* for False in the Answers column to show whether each of the following statements is true or false.

Answers

1. Bartering was a common means of business activity in America from the early 1600s to the mid 1700s. **LO 1-1**

   1._____

2. The industrial revolution in America began in the mid-1800s. **LO 1-1**

   2._____

3. Specialization results in a more efficient economy. **LO 1-1**

   3._____

4. The growth of American cities began hand-in-hand with the rise of the factory system in America. **LO 1-1**

   4._____

5. Between the start of World War I in 1914 until the end of World War II in 1945, the U.S. economy grew at the fastest rate in history. **LO 1-1**

   5._____

6. By the beginning of the twentieth century, American workers were progressing from hand laborers to semi-skilled workers. **LO 1-2**

   6._____

7. Productivity grows if outputs are reduced while inputs are increased. **LO 1-2**

   7._____

8. Brand names gained great importance in the years following World War II. **LO 1-2**

   8._____

9. The so-called "information age" began in the late 1950s as the United States and the Soviet Union battled for supremacy in space exploration. **LO 1-2**

   9._____

10. Business in the information age is characterized more with building relationships with customers than simply with selling goods to customers. **LO 1-2**

    10._____

Part 2 Multiple Choice

Directions: In the Answers column, write the letter that represents the word, or group of words, that correctly completes the statement or answers the question.

Answers

11. Jacob agrees to plough Benjamin's field; in exchange, Benjamin will help Jacob build a new pen for his livestock. Jacob and Benjamin are engaged in _____. (a) buying and selling (b) bartering (c) auctioning (d) branding **LO 1-1**

    11._____

12. The process of making large quantities of goods and services in factories is called _____. (a) globalization (b) mechanization (c) specialization (d) industrialization **LO 1-1**

    12._____

13. *Specialization* occurs when _____. (a) employees use advanced tools and machinery (b) individuals exchange one product for another (c) workers are doing just a few tasks and learning to do them well (d) people make for themselves almost everything they consume **LO 1-1**

    13._____

14. Which of the following statements about the "Gilded Age" is correct? (a) The U.S. economy grew very slowly during this time. (b) New towns were formed and super-rich industrialists emerged. (c) The environmentalist movement had a great impact on business activities during this time. (d) Immigration to the United States slowed to a trickle. **LO 1-1**

    14._____

15. The use of tools and machines is called _____. (a) commercialization (b) mechanization (c) consumerism (d) industrialization **LO 1-2**

    15._____

16. A middle class began to grow in numbers and importance in the United States in _____.   16._____
(a) the early 1900s (b) the years following World War II (c) the early 1960s (d) the
information age **LO 1-2**

17. By the 1950s, _____. (a) fewer people than ever were seeking a college education   17._____
(b) more women began entering the job market than ever before (c) millions of Americans
were leaving their factory jobs and rediscovering farm life (d) all of these **LO 1-2**

18. He introduced the assembly line, which quickly changed the way America made its products.   18._____
(a) Andrew Carnegie (b) Andrew Mellon (c) John D. Rockefeller (d) Henry Ford **LO 1-2**

19. The late 1940s through the 1970s was characterized by _____. (a) widespread   19._____
consumerism (b) a decline in the standard of living for most Americans (c) a return to the
barter system (d) the rise of mass production **LO 1-2**

20. The most important invention of the so-called information age is undoubtedly the _____.   20._____
(a) television (b) automobile (c) computer (d) printing press **LO 1-2**

Part 3 Short Answer

Directions: Read the following questions, and write your response.

21. What is *specialization*? Can you think of any disadvantages to specialization? **LO 1-1**

22. What is different about the way businesses view consumers now, compared to the way they viewed them
during the era of mass production? How does this difference impact your life as a consumer?
LO 1-2

Part 4 Critical Thinking

Directions: Read the following question, and write your response.

23. Do you and your friends have strong feelings about the brands of the products you buy? For example,
maybe you only wear a certain brand of shoe. Or maybe you have to have a certain brand of toothpaste.
In the space below, name one or two brand names you always purchase and explain why. Then name at
least one brand of product that you would *never* buy and tell why. **LO 1-2**

6-2 Proprietorships in America

Part 1 True or False

Directions: Place a *T* for True or an *F* for False in the Answers column to show whether each of the following statements is true or false.

Answers

1. The sole proprietorship is the least common form of business ownership in the United States today. **LO 2-1**　　1. _____

2. All sole proprietorships have only one employee. **LO 2-1**　　2. _____

3. Sole proprietors keep all of the profits of the business. **LO 2-1**　　3. _____

4. *Unlimited liability* means that a proprietor's personal property can be lost if the business fails. **LO 2-2**　　4. _____

5. *Collateral* is assets that have value and can be sold for cash. **LO 2-2**　　5. _____

6. The owner of a business usually works far fewer hours than the employees; this is one of the major advantages to owning one's own business. **LO 2-2**　　6. _____

7. Limited liability companies can be owned by more than one person—not just a single person. **LO 2-3**　　7. _____

8. Unlike sole proprietorships, limited liability companies must hold special annual meetings. **LO 2-3**　　8. _____

9. Limited liability companies are more complex than sole proprietorships. **LO 2-4**　　9. _____

10. In some states, certain businesses cannot form limited liability companies. **LO 2-4**　　10. _____

Part 2 Multiple Choice

Directions: In the Answers column, write the letter that represents the word, or group of words, that correctly completes the statement or answers the question.

Answers

11. With a sole proprietorship, _____. (a) owners may not write off business-related expenses (b) all business earnings are taxed as income of the owner (c) both of these (d) neither of these **LO 2-1**　　11. _____

12. Which of the following statements about a sole proprietorship is *correct*? (a) The sole proprietor makes all the decisions about the company. (b) Sole proprietorships are heavily regulated by government. (c) Sole proprietors must share profits with stockholders. (d) It is very difficult to start a sole proprietorship. **LO 2-1**　　12. _____

13. The most important advantage of a sole proprietorship is probably _____. (a) the independence gained by the owner (b) the ability to finance the business through the sale of stocks (c) limited liability (d) no necessary business licenses to purchase **LO 2-1**　　13. _____

14. Unlimited liability for sole proprietors means that _____. (a) they will find it easy to obtain financing for their business (b) they will not need to provide collateral for business loans (c) they can lose all of their personal assets if the business fails (d) they are in complete control of all of the decisions concerning the business **LO 2-2**　　14. _____

15. Companies that supply products and services to sole proprietors are called _____. (a) partners (b) investors (c) creditors (d) vendors **LO 2-2**　　15. _____

16. To fund his or her business, a sole proprietor often relies on _____. (a) personal bank loans (b) personal lines of credit (c) personal credit cards (d) all of these **LO 2-2**   16._____

17. If the owner of a sole proprietorship dies, _____. (a) the company continues in business under new management (b) by law, the employee with most seniority becomes the new owner (c) that is the end of the company (d) the government will manage the business until a new owner can be found **LO 2-2**   17._____

18. The limited liability company creates a sole proprietorship _____. (a) with the burden of "double taxation" (b) without unlimited liability (c) that requires the owners to distribute profits equally to all employees (d) that is not eligible to take any business tax deductions **LO 2-3**   18._____

19. Limited liability companies can be owned by _____. (a) more than one person (b) other companies (c) foreign investors (d) all of these **LO 2-3**   19._____

20. Unlike the sole proprietorship, _____. (a) annual franchise taxes must be paid to the state where a limited liability company is organized (b) the services of an attorney will probably not be required to set up a limited liability company (c) limited liability companies are authorized to sell stock (d) all of these **LO 2-4**   20._____

Part 3 Short Answer

Directions: Read the following questions, and write your response.

21. Name some reasons why sole proprietorships are so common in the United States. **LO 2-1**

22. How is liability a problem for the owner of a sole proprietorship? How can the owners of a limited liability company avoid this problem? **LO 2-2/LO 2-3**

Part 4 Critical Thinking

Directions: Read the following questions, and write your response.

23. It can sometimes be difficult for sole proprietors to attract top-quality employees. In the space below, speculate about why this is true. **LO 2-2**

24. Name a few of the sole proprietorships located in your community. How many of these do you patronize? **LO 2-1**

Chapter 6 Business Organizations

6-3 Partnerships in America

Part 1 True or False

Directions: Place a *T* for True or an *F* for False in the Answers column to show whether each of the following statements is true or false.

Answers

1. When two or more people go into business together as co-owners, it is called a *partnership*. **LO 3-1**

   1. _____

2. In a general partnership, all partners share in the profits from the business but only one partner is responsible for managing the company. **LO 3-2**

   2. _____

3. A partnership agreement clearly states what each partner has agreed to do. **LO 3-1**

   3. _____

4. Partnerships usually have more available investment than sole proprietorships. **LO 3-1**

   4. _____

5. Unlike a proprietorship, partnerships themselves pay taxes. The partners themselves, however, do not need to file tax returns. **LO 3-1**

   5. _____

6. Limited partners do not share profits with any other partners. **LO 3-2**

   6. _____

7. Limited partners may only contribute money or property to a partnership. **LO 3-2**

   7. _____

8. In a limited partnership, the rights of general partners are the same as they are in a general partnership. **LO 3-2**

   8. _____

9. A limited liability partnership protects only limited partners, not general partners. **LO 3**

   9. _____

10. Limited liability partnerships vary on a state-by-state basis. **LO 3-3**

    10. _____

Part 2 Multiple Choice

Directions: In the Answers column, write the letter that represents the word, or group of words, that correctly completes the statement or answers the question.

Answers

11. Which of the following is *not* one of the three types of partnerships? (a) general partnership (b) limited partnership (c) sole partnership (d) limited liability partnership **LO 3-1**

    11. _____

12. Which of the following statements about partnerships is *correct*? (a) They are easy to start. (b) Government regulations are strict. (c) They are subject to double taxation. (d) all of these **LO 3-1**

    12. _____

13. In the United States, most general partnerships consist of how many partners? (a) one (b) two (c) three (d) more than four **LO 3-1**

    13. _____

14. Janice and Sue are partners in a business. Without Janice's knowledge, Sue enters a business deal that creates a massive debt for the business—and consequently for Janice as well. This is an example of _____. (a) limited liability (b) double indemnity (c) mutual agency (d) partnership fraud **LO 3-1**

    14. _____

15. The most serious disadvantage of a general partnership is _____. (a) partners must share profits (b) unlimited liability of all partners (c) partnerships usually terminate if one partners leaves or a new partner joins (d) disagreements between partners may arise **LO 3-1**

    15. _____

16. The word *limited* in limited partnership refers to the _____. (a) income partners can earn (b) amount of taxes the partnership must pay (c) amount of day-to-day responsibility each partner has (d) extent of partners' liability for loss if the business fails **LO 3-2**

    16. _____

17. Limited partners cannot contribute _____ to the business. (a) money (b) property   17. _____
    (c) personal services (d) any of these **LO 3-2**

18. Which of the following has the *least* personal liability in a business? (a) limited partner   18. _____
    (b) sole proprietor (c) general partner (d) they all have an equal amount of liability **LO 3-2**

19. The main advantage of a limited liability partnership is that it _____. (a) distributes   19. _____
    profits equally (b) does not require a partnership agreement (c) makes it easier for the
    business to attract employees (d) protects all partners **LO 3-3**

20. Which of the following statements about limited liability partnerships is *correct*? (a) Any   20. _____
    type of company can become a limited liability partnership. (b) In an LLP, only one partner
    may take an active role in managing the business. (c) The amount of liability protection
    varies by state. (d) all of these **LO 3-3**

Part 3 Short Answer

Directions: Read the following questions, and write your response.

21. List the items that are covered in a partnership agreement. **LO 3-1**

22. Define the terms *limited partnership* and *limited partner*. **LO 3-2**

23. Name two ways a limited liability partnership and a limited liability company are the same. **LO 3-3**

Part 4 Critical Thinking

Directions: Read the following question, and write your response.

24. Place an X next to each point listed below if it is true for *both* a general partnership and a sole
    proprietorship. Do not check off points that are true for only one form of business organization.
    LO 2-1/3-1

    _____ easy to set up

    _____ enjoyment of profits without having to share them

    _____ one person makes all the decisions and controls what the company does

    _____ easy to attract financing and gain credit

    _____ business itself does not pay taxes

    _____ more efficient operations because of shared responsibilities

    _____ unlimited liability

6-4 Corporations in America

Part 1 True or False

Directions: Place a *T* for True or an *F* for False in the Answers column to show whether each of the following statements is true or false.

Answers

1. Unlike a proprietorship or partnership, a corporation is separate and distinct from its owners. **LO 4-1**

    1. _____

2. The returns to corporation owners of the profits earned by the company are called *interest*. **LO 4-1**

    2. _____

3. Most proprietorships or partnerships become an S corporation in order to avoid unlimited liability. **LO 4-1**

    3. _____

4. Nonprofit corporations do not need to generate income. **LO 4-1**

    4. _____

5. A corporation is born when the paperwork is filed with the state. **LO 4-2**

    5. _____

6. Individuals who purchase common stock have unlimited liability if the corporation goes out of business. **LO 4-2**

    6. _____

7. Preferred stockholders are paid dividends before common stockholders. **LO 4-2**

    7. _____

8. Corporations cease to exist when the CEO retires or dies. **LO 4-3**

    8. _____

9. Because of their large size, it is generally difficult for corporations to find and retain qualified employees. **LO 4-3**

    9. _____

10. In most states, corporations must hold annual meetings of the board of directors. **LO 4-3**

    10. _____

Part 2 Multiple Choice

Directions: In the Answers column, write the letter that represents the word, or group of words, that correctly completes the statement or answers the question.

Answers

11. A C corporation _____. (a) is also referred to as a "family business corporation" (b) is not subject to double taxation (c) sells stock to the public (d) all of these **LO 4-1**

    11. _____

12. All of the following statements about private corporations are true *except* _____. (a) they are closed to public investment (b) they are all very small (c) they are not regulated by the SEC (d) they are usually limited in the number of shares they can sell **LO 4-1**

    12. _____

13. You notice that a business is named Tipton and Henry, Surveyors, PC. This tells you that the business is a(n) _____. (a) nonprofit corporation (b) private corporation (c) S corporation (d) C corporation **LO 4-1**

    13. _____

14. Nonprofit corporations _____. (a) do not pay federal or state income taxes (b) exist to provide a public service of some type (c) do not pay dividends (d) all of these **LO 4-1**

    14. _____

15. The basic rules and procedures that govern how a corporation will operate are called the _____. (a) corporate bylaws (b) partnership agreement (c) articles of incorporation (d) code of ethics **LO 4-2**

    15. _____

16. Owners of corporations are called _____. (a) agents (b) stockholders (c) partners (d) directors **LO 4-2**

    16. _____

17. The day-to-day operations of a corporation are managed by the _____. (a) chief executive 17. _____
officer (b) board of directors (c) stockholders (d) partners **LO 4-2**

18. This is the biggest advantage of corporate ownership. (a) perpetual life (b) double taxation 18. _____
(c) ease of acquiring financing (d) limited liability **LO 4-3**

19. Transfer of ownership in a corporation generally takes place at (a) savings and loan 19. _____
associations (b) stock markets and exchanges (c) board of directors meetings (d) none of
these **LO 4-3**

20. The most highly regulated corporations are _____. (a) nonprofit corporations 20. _____
(b) C corporations (c) S corporations (d) private corporations **LO 4-3**

Part 3 Short Answer

Directions: Read the following questions, and write your response.

21. What is the purpose and function of the Securities and Exchange Commission (SEC)? **LO 3-1**

22. What is the role of a corporation's board of directors? **LO 3-2**

23. What is a stakeholder? Name at least three stakeholders in a typical corporation. **LO 3-3**

Part 4 Critical Thinking

Directions: Read the following question, and write your response.

24. List the advantages and disadvantages of owning common stock and preferred stock. **LO 1-2**

Common Stock		Preferred Stock	
Advantages	**Disadvantages**	**Advantages**	**Disadvantages**

Chapter 6 Business Organizations

Chapter 6 Review

Part 1 True or False

Directions: Place a *T* for True or an *F* for False in the Answers column to show whether each of the following statements is true or false.

Answers

1. Globalization is the process of making large quantities of goods and services in factories. **LO 1-1**

    1._____

2. The standard of living greatly increased for most Americans during the 1950s and 1960s. **LO 1-2**

    2._____

3. Sole proprietors must share all profits with shareholders. **LO 2-1**

    3._____

4. A sole proprietor is fully responsible for all of the business's losses. **LO 2-2**

    4._____

5. There is no cost to create a limited liability company. **LO 2-4**

    5._____

6. A partnership faces many crippling government regulations. **LO 3-1**

    6._____

7. Unlike general partnerships, limited partnerships do not require a partnership agreement. **LO 3-2**

    7._____

8. Numerically, C corporations are fewer than proprietorships and partnerships, but they do a lion's share of business in terms of income. **LO 4-1**

    8._____

9. The filing fees for incorporation are the same no matter the size of the organization. **LO 4-2**

    9._____

10. Corporations are very complex and establishing one can be very expensive. **LO 4-3**

    10._____

Part 2 Multiple Choice

Directions: In the Answers column, write the letter that represents the word, or group of words, that correctly completes the statement or answers the question.

Answers

11. Which of the following economic activities was most important in colonial America? (a) consumerism (b) mechanization (c) specialization (d) barter **LO 1-1**

    11._____

12. The value of outputs compared to the cost of inputs is _____. (a) industrialization (b) productivity (c) differentiation (d) efficiency **LO 1-2**

    12._____

13. Which of the following is a sole proprietor? (a) a salesperson at an electronics store (b) an employee of a bike shop (c) a clothing boutique owner (d) all of these **LO 2-1**

    13._____

14. A limited life is a disadvantage of a(n) _____. (a) C corporation (b) sole proprietorship (c) S corporation (d) private corporation **LO 2-2**

    14._____

15. Teresa knows nothing about lawn mower repair, but she invests in her friend Larry's mower repair business. Larry manages the day-to-day operations and has unlimited liability; both Larry and Teresa share in the profits of the business. This business is most likely a _____. (a) general partnership (b) sole proprietorship (c) limited partnership (d) C corporation **LO 3-1**

    15._____

16. The United Way is an example of a _____. (a) nonprofit corporation (b) private corporation (c) limited partnership (d) sole proprietorship **LO 4-1**

    16._____

17. Corporations can _____. (a) own property (b) borrow money (c) sue and be sued (d) all 17._____
of these **LO 4-1**

18. Most of the major companies in the United States are _____. (a) sole proprietorships 18._____
(b) S corporations (c) C corporations (d) general partnerships **LO 4-1**

19. The paperwork called _____ contains information about a corporation, its owners, its 19._____
purpose, and the stock that will be issued. (a) articles of incorporation (b) partnership
agreement (c) corporate bylaws (d) mission statement **LO 4-2**

20. Which of the following is subjected to double taxation? (a) limited partnership (b) sole 20._____
proprietorship (c) corporation (d) general partnership **LO 4-3**

Part 3 Short Answer

Directions: Read the following questions, and write your response.

21. What are the advantages and disadvantages of sole proprietorships? **LO 2-1/LO 2-2**

22. Briefly explain the concept of "double taxation." **LO 4-1**

Part 4 Critical Thinking

Directions: Read the directions and then fill in the chart.

23. Identify the time period of each of the major eras of American business, and list the major characteristics
of each. **LO 1-1/LO 1-2**

Era	Time Period	Major Characteristics
Colonies		
Factories		
The Gilded Age		
Mass Production		
Consumerism		
Information Age		

Chapter 6 Business Organizations

7-1 Own Your Own Business

Part 1 True or False

Directions: Place a *T* for True or an *F* for False in the Answers column to show whether each of the following statements is true or false.

Answers

1. If you operate a side business, you will likely need to quit your full-time job to devote all of your time to the new venture. **LO 1-1**

1. _____

2. Most side businesses start small but grow large rather quickly. **LO 1-1**

2. _____

3. A lifestyle business usually is operated from an office or specialized business space, not from the owner's home. **LO 1-1**

3. _____

4. A startup business is one where the owner intends to keep the business small. **LO 1-1**

4. _____

5. The business startup company is the most risky type of business. **LO 1-1**

5. _____

6. A nail salon is an example of a service business. **LO 1-2**

6. _____

7. A *target price* involves setting your price at or below that of your competitors. **LO 1-2**

7. _____

8. It is more difficult to obtain business loans if you buy an existing business, as compared to starting an entirely new business. **LO 1-2**

8. _____

9. A *franchise* is a legal contract that gives you the right to sell another company's product or service in a geographic area. **LO 1-2**

9. _____

10. A major advantage of buying a franchise is that the initial franchise fee is refundable if your business fails. **LO 1-2**

10. _____

Part 2 Multiple Choice

Directions: In the Answers column, write the letter that represents the word, or group of words, that correctly completes the statement or answers the question.

Answers

11. A side business _____. (a) often offers specialty goods not available in the regular marketplace (b) typically has limited growth potential (c) is often operated out of the owner's home (d) all of these **LO 1-1**

11. _____

12. For a side business, the most common method of getting customers is _____. (a) word of mouth (b) television and radio advertising (c) door-to-door sales (d) telemarketing **LO 1-1**

12. _____

13. Which of the following statements about lifestyle businesses is *correct*? (a) A lifestyle business is the owner's part-time job. (b) When the owner retires, the business closes. (c) Lifestyle businesses are usually an extension of the owner's hobby or special interest. (d) Lifestyle businesses have strong growth potential. **LO 1-1**

13. _____

14. This type of business may start small, but the owner intends to grow it into a large corporation. (a) lifestyle business (b) startup business (c) side business (d) all of these **LO 1-1**

14. _____

15. Which of the following is an example of *equity financing*? (a) obtaining a business loan from a bank (b) selling corporate bonds (c) getting a loan from a friend (d) selling stock to the public **LO 1-1**

15. _____

16. This type of business buys products, adds a markup, and sells them to consumers. (a) retail business (b) service business (c) manufacturing company (d) wholesaler **LO 1-2**

16. _____

17. Which of the following statements about starting your own company is *correct*? (a) The business already has an existing customer base. (b) It can be hard to predict demand for the products sold by a new business. (c) Customer goodwill can help get the business off the ground. (d) It is easier to obtain financing for a new business than for any other type of business. **LO 1-2**

17. ____

18. If you buy an existing business, _____. (a) you can expect to pay royalties to the previous owner for years to come (b) your initial down payment is refundable if the business does not succeed (c) you will also be buying the equipment and supplies (d) you will not need to worry about keeping customers happy **LO 1-2**

18. ____

19. The _____ is what you pay for the right to operate a franchise. (a) initial franchise fee (b) down payment (c) startup fee (d) royalty fee **LO 1-2**

19. ____

20. One problem with buying a franchise is that _____. (a) most products and services offered by franchises are not well known (b) there is not much of a customer base for most franchises (c) if another franchise does something bad, it can affect your business also (d) you cannot count on much—if any—assistance from the franchise owner **LO 1-2**

20. ____

Part 3 Short Answer

Directions: Read the following questions, and write your response.

21. Name the three main types of small businesses. **LO 1-1**

22. What is an *exit strategy*? **LO 1-1**

23. Which business venture is most risky: starting a business, buying a business, or buying a franchise? Explain your answer. **LO 1-2**

Part 4 Critical Thinking

Directions: Read the directions and then fill in the chart.

24. Enter the words *Low*, *Medium*, or *High* to categorize the costs, features, and benefits of each type of business listed in the table below. **LO 1-1**

Type of Business	Dollar Investment Needed	Risk to Owner	Time Required by Owner	Likelihood of Business Failure	Potential for Great Wealth
Side					
Lifestyle					
Startup					

7-2 Prepare a Business Plan

Part 1 True or False

Directions: Place a *T* for True or an *F* for False in the Answers column to show whether each of the following statements is true or false.

Answers

1. A *business plan* is an oral presentation you make to a potential lender that describes all the things you will do to ensure business success. **LO 2-1**   1._____

2. The information in a business plan is confidential. **LO 2-1**   2._____

3. A business plan can help the owner better visualize exactly what the business needs. **LO 2-1**   3._____

4. Once a business plan has helped an owner obtain financing, the owner does not need to refer to it again. **LO 2-1**   4._____

5. The first part of a business plan is called the Foreword. **LO 2-2**   5._____

6. A business plan should include an explanation of why the business will succeed and how it will be better than the competition. **LO 2-2**   6._____

7. *Location* refers to the physical spot your business will operate and how that will be attractive to customers. **LO 2-2**   7._____

8. The three parts of the Financial section of a business plan are Risk Assessment, Financial Statements, and Operations Management. **LO 2-2**   8._____

9. The Small Business Development Center is a government agency that provides low-interest loans to select new business startups. **LO 2-2**   9._____

10. It is sometimes a good idea to include personal financial statements and tax returns in a business plan. **LO 2-2**   10._____

Part 2 Multiple Choice

Directions: In the Answers column, write the letter that represents the word, or group of words, that correctly completes the statement or answers the question.

Answers

11. Which of the following statements about a business plan is *incorrect*? (a) Business plans assure lenders that business loans will be repaid. (b) Business plans do not need to include information about the skill level of the employees. (c) Business plans outline what the firm will produce, how it will produce, and who will buy it. (d) Business plans should be shared only with those who need access to the information they contain. **LO 2-1**   11._____

12. The most important reason why a new business needs a business plan is to _____. (a) meet the needs of external users (b) to make sure employees know what is expected of them (c) comply with government regulations regarding business startups (d) give the owner a game plan for success **LO 2-1**   12._____

13. *Financing* refers to _____. (a) the profits your business will make over the long run (b) the salaries a business pays its employees (c) the money you need to get your business going and help it stay running (d) the money customers spend for your goods and services **LO 2-1**   13._____

14. A business plan should include _____. (a) business goals and objectives (b) your future plans for the firm (c) an honest assessment of your weaknesses (d) all of these **LO 2-1**   14._____

15. The Introduction section of a business plan _____. (a) should explain who will own the   15._____
company and the ownership structure (b) should be no more than one or two paragraphs
(c) should contain a detailed analysis of the business's financial needs (d) describes the day-
to-day management of the business **LO 2-2**

16. All of the following are included in the Marketing Strategy section of a business plan *except*   16._____
(a) a description of your industry (b) a financial plan (c) an explanation of your business's
location (d) information about the market where you will operate **LO 2-2**

17. This pro forma financial statement estimates your financial position as your business gets   17._____
started and grows. (a) statement of cash flows (b) income statement (c) equity statement
(d) balance sheet **LO 2-2**

18. The term *operations* describes _____. (a) the business's financial needs (b) the day-to-day   18._____
management of the business (c) the overall field of business (d) how your product or service
will be bought and sold **LO 2-2**

19. This is a page-long summary of your entire business plan. (a) purpose statement (b) cover   19._____
letter (c) executive summary (d) title page **LO 2-2**

20. Charts, graphs, documents, and other data that back up information you give in your report   20._____
should be placed in _____. (a) an appendix to the business plan (b) the conclusion
(c) the purpose statement (d) the bibliography to the business plan **LO 2-2**

Part 3 Short Answer

Directions: Read the following questions, and write your response.

21. How can a business owner use a business plan as a "strategy map"? **LO 2-1**

22. What is a cover letter to a business plan? What information is included in a cover letter? **LO 2-2**

Part 4 Critical Thinking

23. Complete the graphic organizer below to show the key information that should be included in each major
section of a business plan. **LO 2-2**

Introduction	Marketing Strategy	Financial Plan	Operations Management	Conclusions

7-3 Succeed in Business

Part 1 True or False

Directions: Place a *T* for True or an *F* for False in the Answers column to show whether each of the following statements is true or false.

Answers

1. Poor planning is a common cause of business failure. **LO 3-1**   1. _____

2. A company that has insufficient capital cannot pay its bills or its employees. **LO 3-1**   2. _____

3. The location of a business usually has little impact on the success of the business. **LO 3-1**   3. _____

4. It may seem unlikely, but a business may be harmed by growing too fast. **LO 3-1**   4. _____

5. Excess inventory is nothing more than a minor inconvenience for a business because the value of the inventory will stay constant. **LO 3-1**   5. _____

6. Successfully starting a business depends largely on the general economy, and economic conditions can change quickly. **LO 3-1**   6. _____

7. When you make and sell a new product with a high profit potential, you will attract competition. **LO 3-1**   7. _____

8. A business with a bad reputation often finds itself unable to attract new customers or even unable to keep existing customers. **LO 3-1**   8. _____

9. Businesses that succeed seem to have very little in common except a focus on providing good quality products and services. **LO 3-2**   9. _____

10. Successful businesses do not need to update or modify their business plans. **LO 3-2**   10. _____

Part 2 Multiple Choice

Directions: In the Answers column, write the letter that represents the word, or group of words, that correctly completes the statement or answers the question.

Answers

11. According to the Small Business Administration, only about half of new businesses survive for _____ years or more. (a) two (b) five (c) ten (d) twenty **LO 3-1**   11. _____

12. In the business sense, the term *capital* refers to _____. (a) money, credit, and other financial resources (b) physical equipment and machinery (c) human resources (d) all of these **LO 3-1**   12. _____

13. How can unexpected growth harm a business's chances of success? (a) Expenses can rise faster than revenue if the firm isn't prepared for the added volume. (b) A new or bigger store can drain profits and lose enough money that the entire business fails. (c) Paying overtime to employees to handle the extra business can reduce profit. (d) All of these. **LO 3-1**   13. _____

14. An accumulated amount of the product that the company provides for sale is called _____. (a) owner's equity (b) assets (c) capital (d) inventory **LO 3-1**   14. _____

15. Because winter was especially mild, a hardware store has thousands of unsold bags of rock salt on hand. This situation is an example of a(n) _____. (a) stock-out (b) unplanned investment (c) unforced investment (d) quantity overload **LO 3-1**   15. _____

16. Gemma's Gaslight Bistro offers cappuccino for $3.00/cup. The Java Hut, located across the street from Gemma's, responds by lowering the price of its cappuccino to $2.90/cup. The next day, a cup costs only $2.75 at Gemma's. Java Hut reduces the price by ten cents more. This is an example of a(n) _____. (a) inventory build-up (b) product overstock (c) price war (d) lack of business ethics on the part of the Java Hut **LO 3-1**

16. _____

17. Business owners can get expert advice and support from _____. (a) the Department of Homeland Security (b) Small Business Development Centers (c) the U.S. Consumer Product Safety Commission (d) all of these **LO 3-2**

17. _____

18. Which of these statements about business startups is *incorrect*? (a) There is never a bad time to start a new business. (b) Sometimes what seems like the worst idea can be successful. (c) Business plans should not be overly optimistic. (d) Getting advice early and often can help prevent business failure. **LO 3-2**

18. _____

19. A successful business sees its business plan as _____. (a) set in stone (b) an unchangeable blueprint for achievement (c) frozen in time (d) a work in progress **LO 3-2**

19. _____

20. A(n) _____ sets out expectations and defines behavior that is acceptable for internal and external business dealings. (a) organization chart (b) business plan (c) ethics policy (d) mission statement **LO 3-2**

20. _____

Part 3 Short Answer

Directions: Read the following questions, and write your response.

21. How can the location of a business affect its success? **LO 3-1**

22. What is a stock-out and how can it prevent a business from succeeding? **LO 3-1**

23. How can business owners realistically assess their chances for success? **LO 3-2**

Part 4 Critical Thinking

Directions: Read the following question, and write your response.

24. Have you ever gone to a retail store to purchase something only to find the store was sold out of the item? Did you find the item elsewhere? How did this incident affect your future purchases? Describe your experiences in the space below. **LO 3-1**

25. Your friend Danielle has begun a pet-sitting business. In the space below, help her write a one-paragraph ethics policy for her business. **LO 3-2**

Chapter 7 Review

Part 1 True or False

Directions: Place a *T* for True or an *F* for False in the Answers column to show whether each of the following statements is true or false.

Answers

1. In a side business, people do something they enjoy and are good at, and the business brings in added income. **LO 1-1** 1._____

2. Selling corporate bonds is an example of debt financing. **LO 1-1** 2._____

3. Many existing businesses are for sale because they are not profitable. **LO 1-2** 3._____

4. If you buy a franchise, you will have to make regular payments—called the *initial franchise fee*—to the franchise owner. **LO 1-2** 4._____

5. A business plan can help a business owner obtain financing. **LO 2-1** 5._____

6. A business plan is a financial tool, but not a management tool. **LO 2-1** 6._____

7. Only internal users need to read your business plan. **LO 2-2** 7._____

8. Excess inventory is a planned investment. **LO 3-1** 8._____

9. A price war occurs when businesses keep lowering prices in order to sell goods. **LO 3-1** 9._____

10. It is better for business plans to be overly optimistic rather than overly pessimistic. **LO 3-2** 10._____

Part 2 Multiple Choice

Directions: In the Answers column, write the letter that represents the word, or group of words, that correctly completes the statement or answers the question.

Answers

11. Shirley is a nurse who loves making quilts. In her spare time, she creates custom-order quilts for friends and associates. She sells about a dozen quilts every year. This can best be described as a _____. (a) startup business (b) franchise (c) side business (d) lifestyle business **LO 1-1** 11._____

12. Which type of business would engage in equity financing? (a) lifestyle business (b) startup business (c) side business (d) all of these **LO 1-1** 12._____

13. General Motors is an example of a _____. (a) wholesaler (b) service business (c) retail business (d) manufacturing company **LO 1-2** 13._____

14. If you purchase a McDonald's franchise, you are a(n) _____. (a) franchisee (b) wholesaler (c) franchisor (d) agent **LO 1-2** 14._____

15. A study to find out what consumers will buy and what price they are willing to pay is called _____. (a) ergonomics (b) demographics (c) secondary research (d) market research **LO 1-2** 15._____

16. A written document that lists the things you will do to ensure business success is called a(n) _____. (a) business plan (b) vision statement (c) code of conduct (d) ethics policy **LO 2-1** 16._____

17. A well-written business plan can _____. (a) help an owner rethink certain aspects of the business (b) convince others to work with your business (c) provide strategies for making good business decisions (d) all of these **LO 2-1** 17._____

18. This part of your business plan's Introduction explains whether or not your firm will be a proprietorship, partnership, or corporation. (a) business description (b) skills, experience, and strengths (c) ownership and structure (d) advantages **LO 2-2**

18._____

19. Which of these is a good explanation of a *pro forma financial statement*? (a) It is based on the previous years' results. (b) It is a hypothetical financial statement that forecasts what may happen in the future. (c) It is more accurate than a traditional financial statement. (d) It is not a useful tool for obtaining business financing. **LO 2-2**

19._____

20. Common reasons for business failure include _____. (a) poor planning (b) insufficient capital (c) unexpected growth (d) all of these **LO 3-1**

20._____

Part 3 Short Answer

Directions: Read the following questions, and write your response.

21. What is an executive summary? When should it be used with a business plan? **LO 2-2**

22. How can an ethics policy help a business succeed? **LO 3-2**

Part 4 Critical Thinking

Directions: Answer the following question.

23. In the space below, write the names of the various businesses you have patronized over the past week. Indicate whether the business was a service business or a retail business. If it was also a franchise, underline the name of the business. **LO 1-2**

Service Businesses	Retail Businesses

8-1 What Makes Money *Money*?

Part 1 True or False

Directions: Place a *T* for True or an *F* for False in the Answers column to show whether each of the following statements is true or false.

Answers

1. Exchange cannot occur in an economy without money. **LO 1-1** 1. ____

2. Money is anything that people accept as payment for goods and services. **LO 1-1** 2. ____

3. The medium of exchange function of money provides a common measurement of the value for goods and services. **LO 1-1** 3. ____

4. Credit cards are not considered money. **LO 1-1** 4. ____

5. The ideal money should have an unlimited supply. **LO 1-1** 5. ____

6. The money used in the United States today would be considered commodity money. **LO 1-1** 6. ____

7. M1 is the narrowest definition of the money supply. **LO 1-2** 7. ____

8. Currency represents about half of M1. **LO 1-2** 8. ____

9. The only difference between M1 and M2 is that M2 also consists of checkable deposits. **LO 1-2** 9. ____

10. There is no difference between a checkable deposit and a time deposit. **LO 1-2** 10. ____

Part 2 Multiple Choice

Directions: In the Answers column, write the letter that represents the word, or group of words, that correctly completes the statement or answers the question.

Answers

11. The barter system _____. (a) can be used to exchange goods but not services (b) is relatively inefficient (c) became widespread after the introduction of fiat money (d) all of these **LO 1-1** 11. ____

12. Which of the following could be used as money? (a) animal skins (b) shells (c) precious metals (d) all of these **LO 1-1** 12. ____

13. Which function of money provides a common measurement of value for goods and services? (a) medium of exchange (b) portability (c) unit of account (d) store of value **LO 1-1** 13. ____

14. Credit cards _____ considered money because they _____. (a) are not; do not meet the *medium of exchange* criterion (b) are not; do not meet the *store of value* criterion (c) are; meet the *portability* criterion (d) are; meet the *scarcity* criterion **LO 1-1** 14. ____

15. Ideally, money should be _____. (a) made of precious metals (b) indivisible (c) of uniform quality (d) plentiful **LO 1-1** 15. ____

16. Money accepted by law, and not because of its tangible value, is called _____. (a) fiat money (b) token money (c) commodity money (d) real money **LO 1-1** 16. ____

17. Currency is _____. (a) anything people accept as payment for goods and services (b) anything that serves as money that has market value based on the material from which it is made (c) the same thing as a "demand deposit" (d) coins and paper money **LO 1-2** 17. ____

18. M1 makes up about _____ of M2. (a) 12 percent (b) 22 percent (c) 50 percent (d) 75   18. ____
   percent **LO 1-2**

19. M1 includes _____. (a) currency held by the public (b) savings deposits (c) small time   19. ____
   deposits (d) all of these **LO 1-2**

20. A time deposit is _____. (a) an interest bearing account that can be easily withdrawn   20. ____
   (b) money in a financial institution that can be withdrawn by writing a check (c) an account
   with guaranteed interest for a period of time (d) very similar to a demand deposit **LO 1-2**

Part 3 Short Answer

Directions: Read the following questions, and write your response.

21. What does the term *store of value* mean in relation to money? **LO 1-1**

22. In the space below, give the formulas for both M1 and M2. **LO 1-2**

Part 4 Critical Thinking

Directions: Read the following question, and write your response.

23. The textbook identifies several desirable properties of money. In the space below, speculate about the
   disadvantages of each property if pebbles were used as money. Are there any advantages? **LO 1-1**

Portable	
Divisible	
Uniform	
Scarce	

8-2 How Banks Create Money

Part 1 True or False

Directions: Place a *T* for True or an *F* for False in the Answers column to show whether each of the following statements is true or false.

Answers

1. Banking transactions expand or contract the money supply. **LO 2-1**
    1. _____

2. In the Middle Ages, gold was the money of choice in most European nations. **LO 2-1**
    2. _____

3. Banks can create money by making loans in a 100 percent reserve system. **LO 2-1**
    3. _____

4. The two sides of a bank's balance sheet must always be equal. **LO 2-1**
    4. _____

5. The minimum balance of money that the Fed requires a bank to hold in cash or on deposit with the Fed are called *excess reserves*. **LO 2-1**
    5. _____

6. The Federal Reserve System is the central banking system of the United States. **LO 2-1**
    6. _____

7. First National Bank gives Martin a loan of $10,000. The bank gives him a check for this amount, which he deposits in his account with the bank. The bank's liabilities just increased by $10,000. **LO 2-1**
    7. _____

8. The process of money creation occurs only once, with the original loan. **LO 2-2**
    8. _____

9. Suppose the money multiplier is 10. In this case, an initial deposit of $100,000 would increase M1 by $1 million. **LO 2-2**
    9. _____

10. $\Delta M1 = \Delta ER \times MM$. **LO 2-2**
    10. _____

Part 2 Multiple Choice

Directions: In the Answers column, write the letter that represents the word, or group of words, that correctly completes the statement or answers the question.

Answers

11. Fractional reserve banking originated with _____. (a) Renaissance-era European monarchs (b) medieval goldsmiths (c) the barter system (d) transactions between merchants in ancient Mesopotamia **LO 2-1**
    11. _____

12. Getting a loan increases the size of _____. (a) the reserve requirement (b) the money multiplier (c) checkable deposits (d) all of these **LO 2-1**
    12. _____

13. The amounts a bank owes to others are called _____. (a) credits (b) required reserves (c) liabilities (d) assets **LO 2-1**
    13. _____

14. M1 does not change until _____. (a) a bank makes a loan (b) the reserve requirement is raised (c) a bank accepts a new deposit (d) a bank customer makes a withdrawal from her savings account **LO 2-1**
    14. _____

15. A bank has $40 million in checkable deposits. If the RRR is 10 percent, then required reserves are _____ and excess reserves are _____. (a) $10 million; $30 million (b) $36 million; $4 million (c) $30 million; $10 million (d) $4 million; $36 million **LO 2-1**
    15. _____

16. Which of the following would *not* be listed on the Assets side of a bank's balance sheet? (a) required reserves (b) checkable deposits (c) excess reserves (d) loans **LO 2-1**
    16. _____

17. This type of loan involves greater risks of non-payment by borrowers. (a) sub-prime loans (b) commercial loans (c) prime loans (d) fixed-interest loans **LO 2-1**
    17. _____

18. The _____ gives the maximum change in the money supply due to an initial change in the excess reserves held by banks. (a) required reserve ratio (b) money multiplier (c) balance sheet (d) equilibrium point **LO 2-2**

18. _____

19. The money multiplier has a(n) _____ relationship to the reserve requirement. (a) neutral (b) positive (c) direct (d) inverse **LO 2-2**

19. _____

20. The money multiplier is equal to _____. (a) 1 divided by the required reserve ratio (b) 1 divided by excess reserves (c) assets − liabilities (d) excess reserves divided by ΔM1 **LO 2-2**

20. _____

Part 3 Short Answer

Directions: Read the following questions, and write your response.

21. How does fractional reserve banking allow banks to increase the money supply? **LO 2-1**

22. What is the formula for total reserves? **LO 2-2**

Part 4 Critical Thinking

Directions: Read the following questions, and write your response.

23. How would an increase in the reserve ratio affect a bank? **LO 2-1**

24. If the required reserve ratio is 15 percent, what is the money multiplier? **LO 2-2**

Chapter 8 Review

Part 1 True or False

Directions: Place a *T* for True or an *F* for False in the Answers column to show whether each of the following statements is true or false.

Answers

1. Barter is the direct exchange of one good or service for another good or service, rather than for money. **LO 1-1**

2. The unit of account function of money is the ability of money to hold value over time. **LO 1-1**

3. Today, U.S. paper money and coins are no longer backed by gold or silver. **LO 1-1**

4. Checkable deposits are considered part of M1 but not part of M2. **LO 1-2**

5. There is a difference between a demand deposit and a time deposit. **LO 1-2**

6. An individual bank can lend more than its excess reserves. **LO 2-1**

7. When the reserve ratio is increased, banks are able to increase their lending. **LO 2-1**

8. In the Middle Ages, goldsmith receipts began being used as paper money. **LO 2-1**

9. The higher the reserve requirement, the larger the money multiplier. **LO 2-2**

10. In order to determine the change in the money supply initiated by an initial deposit, you need to calculate all the individual bank transactions associated with the deposit. **LO 2-2**

1. _____
2. _____
3. _____
4. _____
5. _____
6. _____
7. _____
8. _____
9. _____
10. _____

Part 2 Multiple Choice

Directions: In the Answers column, write the letter that represents the word, or group of words, that correctly completes the statement or answers the question.

Answers

11. All of these are considered to be a function of money *except* _____. (a) a unit of account (b) a store of value (c) an indicator of status (d) a medium of exchange **LO 1-1**

12. People should be able to reach into their pockets and make change to buy items at various prices. In other words, money needs to be _____. (a) uniform (b) portable (c) scarce (d) aesthetically pleasing **LO 1-1**

13. Which of the following is an example of commodity money? (a) diamonds (b) silver bars (c) salt (d) all of these **LO 1-1**

14. Time deposits of less than _____ are considered small and therefore are included in M2. (a) $1,000 (b) $10,000 (c) $100,000 (d) $1,000,000 **LO 1-2**

15. Which of the following statements about savings deposits is *correct*? (a) They have a specific maturity date. (b) Withdrawals are penalized. (c) They earn interest. (d) all of these **LO 1-2**

16. Which of the following statements about M1 is *correct*? (a) M1 is a very broad measure of the money supply. (b) M1 measures purchasing power immediately available to the public without borrowing. (c) M1 does not include coins and paper money. (d) all of these **LO 1-2**

17. Banks operating in a fractional reserve banking system _____. (a) keep only a percentage of their deposits on reserve and lend out the remainder (b) are unable to increase the money supply (c) never make loans (d) none of these **LO 2-1**

11. _____
12. _____
13. _____
14. _____
15. _____
16. _____
17. _____

18. The _____ is the percentage of deposits that the Fed requires a bank to hold in cash or on   18. _____
deposit with the Fed rather than being loaned. (a) required reserve ratio (b) money multiplier
ratio (c) liquidity ratio (d) deposit insurance ratio **LO 2-1**

19. If the money multiplier is 5, then an initial deposit of $10,000 would increase M1 by   19. _____
(a) $10,000 (b) $40,000 (c) $50,000 (d) $90,000 **LO 2-2**

20. Which of these factors directly affect the formula for the money multiplier? (a) printing of   20. _____
additional paper money by the U.S. government (b) total amount of demand deposits held by
a bank (c) required reserve ratio (d) all of these **LO 2-2**

Part 3 Short Answer

Directions: Read the following questions, and write your response.

21. What is the purpose of currency? **LO 1-2**

22. Explain the differences between required reserves, excess reserves, and total reserves. **LO 2-1**

Part 4 Critical Thinking

Directions: Read the following question, and write your response.

23. Early in the twentieth century, many of the paper bills in circulation in the United States were "silver
certificates." This meant that the U.S. government offered to redeem them for silver if anyone wanted
them redeemed. Would you consider a silver certificate to be commodity money? Why or why not?
LO 1-1

9-1 Individual Checking and Savings

Part 1 True or False

Directions: Place a *T* for True or an *F* for False in the Answers column to show whether each of the following statements is true or false.

Answers

1. Financial institutions are businesses that provide banking services to consumers and businesses. **LO 1-1**

   1._____

2. You make deposits to your account using a bank signature form. **LO 1-1**

   2._____

3. Deposits in transit have not yet cleared your account, meaning the money has not been deposited into your account. **LO 1-1**

   3._____

4. A savings account usually has fewer restrictions than a checking account. **LO 1-2**

   4._____

5. The most important rule for saving money is to allow your spending to keep pace with your income. **LO 1-2**

   5._____

6. Low-risk investments pay less interest than higher-risk investments. **LO 1-2**

   6._____

7. A safe deposit box is a secure container in a bank's vault that customers can use to store important documents and other small items. **LO 1-3**

   7._____

8. A debit card is the same as an ATM card. **LO 1-3**

   8._____

9. It is illegal for banks to charge customers a fee for providing account services. **LO 1-3**

   9._____

10. When you withdraw and deposit money to your accounts at an ATM owned by your bank, there is usually no charge. **LO 1-3**

    10._____

Part 2 Multiple Choice

Directions: In the Answers column, write the letter that represents the word, or group of words, that correctly completes the statement or answers the question.

Answers

11. Which of the following would not be considered a financial institution? (a) commercial bank (b) insurance agency (c) savings and loan (d) credit union **LO 1-1**

    11._____

12. A _____ check is one that has been approved by the bank or financial institution and all of the involved accounts have been credited or debited. (a) cancelled (b) final (c) bounced (d) cleared **LO 1-1**

    12._____

13. The process of verifying the amount in your checking account matches the bank's record of the amount in the account is called _____. (a) verification (b) resolution (c) reconciliation (d) authentication **LO 1-1**

    13._____

14. This document is used to establish your identity as an account holder. (a) transit slip (b) bank signature form (c) deposit ticket (d) personal identification sheet **LO 1-1**

    14._____

15. The earnings you receive on your balance in a savings account is called _____. (a) income (b) dividends (c) collateral (d) interest **LO 1-2**

    15._____

16. An investment of a fixed sum at a fixed rate of interest for a fixed period of time is called a _____. (a) certificate of deposit (b) money market fund (c) debenture (d) savings bond **LO 1-2**

    16._____

17. If you want to save money, you should follow all of the following rules *except* _____.   17._____
(a) always spend less than you make (b) never deposit money into accounts that pay high
interest rates because these accounts are very risky (c) do not make withdrawals from your
account (d) make sure your savings are insured **LO 1-2**

18. With a(n) _____, the bank is authorized not to honor a check or electronic withdrawal you   18._____
previously wrote or authorized. (a) service fee (b) reconciliation form (c) stop payment
(d) overdraft order **LO 1-3**

19. This is a check that is debited from your checking account when it is written. (a) cashier's   19._____
check (b) money order (c) banker's check (d) commercial check **LO 1-3**

20. Mary has only $125 in her checking account, but she writes a check for $300. Mary has   20._____
written a(n) _____. (a) kited check (b) fraudulent check (c) money order (d) bounced
check **LO 1-3**

Part 3 Short Answer

Directions: Read the following questions, and write your response.

21. What is the formula for simple interest? How much interest would you earn on an initial $500 deposit if
the interest rate was 5% and the time was 6 months? **LO 1-2**

22. What is a money order? Who typically uses money orders? **LO 1-3**

Part 4 Critical Thinking

Directions: Read the following question, and follow the directions.

23. Use the blank check below to show how Rose Dawson would write a check to Kramer's Grocery for
$54.38. Use today's date. **LO 1-1**

```
Rose K. Dawson                                      1125
7811 Moss Ct.
Cincinnati, OH 45236
                              Date _____ 20____

Pay to the order of _____ $ [      ]

_____ Dollars

For _____      _____

   123456789  00123456  1125
```

9-2 Business Banking and Capital Markets

Part 1 True or False

Directions: Place a *T* for True or an *F* for False in the Answers column to show whether each of the following statements is true or false.

Answers

1. Many commercial banks specialize in business customer accounts, and some special services are offered to businesses. **LO 2-1**
   1._____

2. Business accounts must maintain balances in their checking accounts sufficient to meet their expenses to vendors, creditors, and employees. **LO 2-1**
   2._____

3. The fee schedule for business bank accounts is the same as for consumer bank accounts. **LO 2-1**
   3._____

4. Businesses often need loans to get through peak seasons, and they are able to pay off the loans as they go through the valley seasons. **LO 2-1**
   4._____

5. Businesses bring revenue to the bank when they process their sales transactions through the bank. **LO 2-1**
   5._____

6. Businesses typically pay higher rates to borrow money than do consumers. **LO 2-1**
   6._____

7. Business loans are usually pre-arranged with a financial institution, similar to lines of credit. **LO 2-1**
   7._____

8. As consumers and businesses save money, it is then made available for loans. **LO 2-2**
   8._____

9. The interest rate charged to business customers is lower than the rate of interest that a bank pays to its customers who save money. **LO 2-2**
   9._____

10. Interest paid for loans to conduct business is tax deductible. **LO 2-2**
    10._____

Part 2 Multiple Choice

Directions: In the Answers column, write the letter that represents the word, or group of words, that correctly completes the statement or answers the question.

Answers

11. A sweep account _____. (a) is available to both businesses and consumers (b) is used to cover a minimum balance in a checking account (c) does not pay interest (d) all of these **LO 2-1**
    11._____

12. Banks charge fees to business accounts based on _____. (a) services provided (b) balances maintained (c) neither of these (d) both of these **LO 2-1**
    12._____

13. A pre-arranged credit line allows a business to _____. (a) receive interest-free loans from a bank (b) access funds as needed (c) receive deposits of loan funds and other types of financing (d) avoid paying late fees on loan payments **LO 2-1**
    13._____

14. The concept of having an ongoing group of services with a bank is called _____. (a) financial linkage (b) cafeteria investing (c) relationship banking (d) liaisoning **LO 2-1**
    14._____

15. A production loan _____. (a) is made when a consumer borrows money to buy something (b) is more risky than a consumption loan (c) is used to buy something that will help repay the loan (d) all of these **LO 2-1**
    15._____

16. Which of these loans will probably have the lowest interest rate? (a) The Carter Corporation   16._____
    borrows money to purchase a new delivery truck. (b) Alice borrows money to pay for her
    vacation to Mexico. (c) Vicente borrows money to buy a new washer and dryer. (d) all of
    these loans will have the same interest rate **LO 2-1**

17. Banks lend money to businesses from the bank's _____ reserves. (a) total (b) excess   17._____
    (c) required (d) composite **LO 2-2**

18. Which of the following statements about capital markets is *incorrect*? (a) Savings subtract   18._____
    from the capital market. (b) Capital markets exist where businesses are able to go to finance
    operations as well as large purchases. (c) Financial institutions represent a large segment of
    the capital market. (d) Banks are not the only source of money for businesses in the capital
    market. **LO 2-2**

19. Commercial paper _____. (a) is a form of long-term borrowing (b) is not considered part   19._____
    of the capital market (c) involves on corporation borrowing from the excess cash of another
    corporation (d) all of these **LO 2-2**

20. Businesses can take advantage of business deductions and write-offs under the _____.   20._____
    (a) Urban Enterprise Zone Act (b) Small Business Jobs Act (c) Recovery Act (d) Internal
    Revenue Service Tax Code **LO 2-1**

Part 3 Short Answer

Directions: Read the following questions, and write your response.

21. What is the difference between a production loan and a consumption loan? Which is more risky? Why?
    LO 2-1

22. How do business loans contribute to the profit a bank makes? **LO 2-2**

Part 4 Critical Thinking

Directions: Read the following question, and write your response.

23. A local community agrees to exempt property tax payments for manufacturers and developers over the
    next 30 years to entice the businesses to locate or expand to the area. Some residential property owners
    are upset over this, especially because their property tax bills have increased 15 percent over the past
    year. In the space below, explain why the tax exemptions for business are a good or bad idea. **LO 2-1**

9-3 Labor Movements and Markets

Part 1 True or False

Directions: Place a *T* for True or an *F* for False in the Answers column to show whether each of the following statements is true or false.

Answers

1. As America moved from an agricultural nation to an industrial nation in the late 1700s to the mid-1800s, demand for labor remained quite low. **LO 3-1**　　1. _____

2. The term *work conditions* refers to the nature of the workplace and what is required for workers to succeed. **LO 3-1**　　2. _____

3. At the turn of the twentieth century, employers were required by law to pay a "living wage" to all employees. **LO 3-1**　　3. _____

4. Young children worked long hours in factories in the 1800s before laws were made to monitor child labor. **LO 3-1**　　4. _____

5. Collective bargaining seeks to protect workers from unfair practices, as well as provide better pay and more favorable working conditions. **LO 3-2**　　5. _____

6. The first major labor union in the United States was organized in 1886. **LO 3-2**　　6. _____

7. As a result of the Chicago Haymarket Riot in the late 1800s, membership in the Knights of Labor grew quickly from a few thousand members to more than 800,000 members. **LO 3-2**　　7. _____

8. Formed in 1938, The Congress of Industrial Organizations (CIO) was an example of a craft union. **LO 3-2**　　8. _____

9. The National Labor Relations Board was given the power to investigate unfair labor practices. **LO 3-2**　　9. _____

10. Some critics of labor unions argue that they keep wages and benefits artificially high. **LO 3-2**　　10. _____

Part 2 Multiple Choice

Directions: In the Answers column, write the letter that represents the word, or group of words, that correctly completes the statement or answers the question.

Answers

11. Which of the following statements about working conditions in the early 1900s is *correct*? (a) few jobs offered benefits (b) most sick days and vacation days were unpaid (c) most employers allowed workers occasional time away from the job (d) all of these **LO 3-1**　　11. _____

12. Which of the following gave the federal government responsibility for monitoring child labor in the United States? (a) establishment of the Children's Bureau in 1912 (b) passage of the Factory Act in 1833 (c) development of the Congress of Industrial Organizations in 1938 (d) passage of the Norris-LaGuardia Act in 1932 **LO 3-1**　　12. _____

13. Health insurance coverage provided by employers first became common in the _____. (a) 1890s (b) 1920s (c) 1950s (d) 1990s **LO 3-1**　　13. _____

14. The first major labor union in the U.S. was the _____. (a) United Workers of America (b) Knights of Labor (c) National Workers Union (d) U.S. Federation of Labor **LO 3-2**　　14. _____

15. A legal action of a union where members refuse to work until a labor agreement is reached is called a(n) _____. (a) injunction (b) strike (c) boycott (d) insurrection **LO 3-2**   15. ____

16. The American Federation of Labor was headed by _____. (a) Fiorello H. LaGuardia (b) John L. Lewis (c) Eugene V. Debs (d) Samuel Gompers **LO 3-2**   16. ____

17. A union that is based on groups of workers in the same or similar trades is called a(n) _____. (a) closed shop (b) industrial union (c) craft union (d) open shop **LO 3-2**   17. ____

18. What did the Wagner Act do? (a) cut back on courts' ability to stop strikes (b) required employers to act in good faith in collective bargaining (c) reinforced workers' rights to form unions and engage in collective bargaining (d) all of these **LO 3-2**   18. ____

19. Which of these resulted in a growth in union membership and increased power of unions in the workplace? (a) the Haymarket Riot of 1886 (b) passage of the Taft-Hartley Act in 1947 (c) the air traffic controller strike of 1981 (d) creation of the National Labor Relations Board in 1935 **LO 3-2**   19. ____

20. A business that is required by union contract to hire only union members is called a(n) _____. (a) closed shop (b) targeted firm (c) union shop (d) restricted business **LO 3-2**   20. ____

Part 3 Short Answer

Directions: Read the following questions, and write your response.

21. Describe working conditions in the typical American factory of the 1800s. **LO 3-1**

22. Provide a brief definition of *collective bargaining*. Who are the parties in a collective bargaining agreement? **LO 3-2**

23. Explain the difference between a craft union, an industrial union, and a public employee union. **LO 3-2**

Part 4 Critical Thinking

Directions: Read the following question, and write your response.

24. Are labor unions still beneficial in a twenty-first century economy? Defend your answer in the space below. **LO 3-2**

Chapter 9 Review

Part 1 True or False

Directions: Place a *T* for True or an *F* for False in the Answers column to show whether each of the following statements is true or false.

Answers

1. A checking account is a demand deposit account where you can make withdrawals and deposit money. **LO 1-1**

   1._____

2. When interest is added to the principal, you will then be earning interest on interest— otherwise known as *simple interest*. **LO 1-2**

   2._____

3. A certificate of deposit is a slightly riskier investment than a regular savings account. **LO 1-2**

   3._____

4. The bank assumes responsibility for paying a cashier's check. **LO 1-3**

   4._____

5. When a business borrows money, it is called a consumption loan. **LO 2-1**

   5._____

6. One reason for business tax incentives is to encourage capital investments by businesses. **LO 2-2**

   6._____

7. Working conditions for children improved in Great Britain long before they improved for children in America. **LO 3-1**

   7._____

8. Factory workers in the 1800s routinely put in 20 or more hours a day on the job, and workers were grateful to have the work. **LO 3-1**

   8._____

9. Labor unions began to form in the United States shortly after the end of the Civil War. **LO 3-2**

   9._____

10. Because of the presence of labor unions, even many non-union employers pay workers competitive wages and benefits. **LO 3-2**

    10._____

Part 2 Multiple Choice

Directions: In the Answers column, write the letter that represents the word, or group of words, that correctly completes the statement or answers the question.

Answers

11. What is the first step of the reconciliation process? (a) deposit funds into your checking account (b) contact your bank to discuss the discrepancy in your account (c) add deposits in transit to the reconciliation form (d) enter the ending balance as shown by the bank on the bank statement on the reconciliation form **LO 1-1**

    11._____

12. In three months, Marissa wants to buy a new sofa. She decides to begin saving $50 each week toward the purchase. Which of these would be the best place for her to deposit her money? (a) an investment account (b) a savings account (c) a one-year certificate of deposit (d) all of these would be equally good choices **LO 1-2**

    12._____

13. Internet banking _____. (a) allows you 24-hour access to your accounts (b) lets you check your account balances (c) permits you to pay bills electronically (d) all of these **LO 1-3**

    13._____

14. An NSF fee is also known as a(n) _____. (a) service fee (b) overdraft charge (c) stop payment charge (d) monthly account fee **LO 1-3**

    14._____

15. Suppose there is a 15% reserve requirement. If a customer has savings of $1000, the bank can create a loan for _____. (a) $850 (b) $150 (c) $800 (d) $100 **LO 2-2**

    15._____

16. In the 1800s, children as young as _____ years old commonly worked _____ hours   16._____
per day in American factories. (a) twelve; six (b) ten; ten (c) six; twelve (d) four; ten **LO 3-1**

17. One reason why Henry Ford's workers were so loyal to him was that _____. (a) he paid   17._____
for the education of his employees' children (b) he offered employees a full slate of paid
benefits, such as vacation and health insurance (c) he worked closely with labor unions to
ensure good working conditions for his employees (d) he paid twice the wage rate of his
competitors **LO 3-1**

18. The Landrum-Griffin Act _____. (a) made union shops illegal (b) limited the ability of   18._____
unions to strike (c) prohibited former convicts from holding office in labor unions (d) set up
the National Labor Relations Board **LO 3-2**

19. He was the first leader of the AFL-CIO. (a) John L. Lewis (b) George Meany (c) Jimmy   19._____
Hoffa (d) Robert Taft **LO 3-2**

20. A union of employees who work for the city, county, state, or federal government is called   20._____
a(n) _____. (a) public employee union (b) administrative union (c) public works union
(d) credit union **LO 3-2**

Part 3 Short Answer

Directions: Read the following questions, and write your response.

21. Why is a checking account called a *demand deposit*? **LO 1-1**

22. Why do businesses need sweep accounts? **LO 2-1**

23. What is an *injunction*? **LO 3-2**

Part 4 Critical Thinking

Directions: Read the following question, and write your response.

24. The last half of the twentieth century witnessed a decline in overall union membership, resulting in less
union power in the workplace by the 1990s. In the space below, identify at least four specific events that
helped lead to this change of fortune for the American labor movement. **LO 3-2**

10-1 Consumer Buying and Credit

Part 1 True or False

Directions: Place a *T* for True or an *F* for False in the Answers column to show whether each of the following statements is true or false.

Answers

1. Impulse buying ensures that you are buying goods and services that will best meet your needs at the lowest possible cost. **LO 1-1**   1._____

2. When you make a major purchase or spend a large sum of money, a buying plan will help you do a thorough analysis before you buy. **LO 1-1**   2._____

3. A spending limit is a pre-set amount that you will pay for an item. **LO 1-1**   3._____

4. Sometimes the right purchasing decision involves *not* buying. **LO 1-1**   4._____

5. Credit decreases your standard of living. **LO 1-2**   5._____

6. If you have successfully used credit in the past, you can more easily get credit in the future when you need it. **LO 1-2**   6._____

7. You will pay more for purchases you have charged to your credit card unless you pay off the entire amount of your credit card bill each month. **LO 1-2**   7._____

8. One major disadvantage of credit is that it is difficult to verify your purchases and make returns. **LO 1-2**   8._____

9. It is illegal for creditors to impose higher interest rates on consumers who have a history of making late credit payments. **LO 1-3**   9._____

10. If you cannot make a credit payment, you should contact the creditor and explain why you need to delay the payments. **LO 1-3**   10._____

Part 2 Multiple Choice

Directions: In the Answers column, write the letter that represents the word, or group of words, that correctly completes the statement or answers the question.

Answers

11. This occurs when you buy something on the spot, without thinking about it. (a) reflex buying (b) impulse buying (c) planned purchasing (d) automatic acquiring **LO 1-1**   11._____

12. Which of the following is an example of buyer's remorse? (a) Polly went into the stereo shop for a new pair of speakers and walked out with a $5000 sound system. Two days later, she was sorry she made the purchase. (b) Garth carefully researched all possible automobiles until he found one that best met his needs. He loves his new car. (c) At the checkout line, Midori grabbed a candy bar to eat on the way home from the grocery. She bought one for her sister, too. (d) none of these **LO 1-1**   12._____

13. Once you decide what your buying goal is, the next step is to _____. (a) research your options (b) make a list of important criteria (c) set a spending limit (d) make the purchase decision **LO 1-1**   13._____

14. You can avoid buying items you don't really need if you _____. (a) always pay with a credit card (b) use a buying plan (c) only buy products your friends recommend (d) all of these **LO 1-1**   14._____

15. Which of these statements about credit is *correct*? (a) carrying a credit card is more dangerous than carrying cash (b) using credit reduces your buying power (c) credit frees up future income (d) credit can pay you back with cash or other rewards **LO 1-2**   15._____

16. The process of looking for the best value for the money spent is called _____. (a) planned purchasing (b) comparison shopping (c) pro-and-con shopping (d) rebating **LO 1-2**   16._____

17. Which of the following is a *financing option*? (a) borrowing from a credit union (b) paying for a purchase with cash (c) using a credit card (d) all of these **LO 1-2**   17._____

18. If you do not make a credit payment on time, you may be charged a(n) _____. (a) NSF fee (b) overdraft penalty (c) late fee (d) overdue penalty **LO 1-3**   18._____

19. Chantal's credit card allows her to charge up to $2500. If she charges $3000 this month, she will be charged a(n) _____. (a) over-the-limit fee (b) insufficient funds fee (c) late fee (d) overage penalty **LO 1-3**   19._____

20. Gunter noticed a charge on his credit card bill that he did not make. In this situation, Gunter should _____. (a) simply ignore the charge because he did not make the error (b) write a letter to the credit card company to dispute the charge (c) call the credit card company to discuss the matter (d) immediately cancel his account with the credit card company **LO 1-3**   20._____

Part 3 Short Answer

Directions: Read the following questions, and write your response.

21. Explain how credit can reduce your future spending and saving power. **LO 1-2**

22. Name at least four responsibilities you have as a user of credit. **LO 1-3**

Part 4 Critical Thinking

Directions: Read the following questions, and write your response.

23. Have you ever felt buyer's remorse? Describe the incident and tell what you might have done differently to prevent it. **LO 1-1**

24. What do you consider the biggest disadvantages of credit? Explain. **LO 1-2**

10-2 Consumer Loans and Credit Scores

Part 1 True or False

Directions: Place a *T* for True or an *F* for False in the Answers column to show whether each of the following statements is true or false.

Answers

1. People who are willing to make loans are called *debtors*. **LO 2-1** 1._____

2. A single-payment loan gives you use of the full amount borrowed for the entire time of the loan. **LO 2-1** 2._____

3. A *co-signer* is a person who also signs a loan agreement and agrees to pay the loan if the borrower is unable to do so. **LO 2-1** 3._____

4. *Service credit* is a type of credit businesses extend to other businesses, such as vendors and suppliers. It is not available to consumers. **LO 2-1** 4._____

5. Credit card and store accounts are a type of secured debt. **LO 2-1** 5._____

6. A charge card is a type of revolving credit. **LO 2-1** 6._____

7. Credit unions are businesses that gather, store, and sell credit information about consumers to their business members. **LO 2-2** 7._____

8. You have a legal right to see your credit report, although you may be charged a fee. **LO 2-2** 8._____

9. You cannot be turned down for credit if your FICO score is in the 700s or higher. **LO 2-2** 9._____

10. Using too much of the same type of credit will lower your overall credit score. **LO 2-2** 10._____

Part 2 Multiple Choice

Directions: In the Answers column, write the letter that represents the word, or group of words, that correctly completes the statement or answers the question.

Answers

11. Under the terms of Dimitri's loan, he makes a $200 payment each month for 12 months. This is an example of a(n) _____. (a) single-payment loan (b) installment loan (c) payday loan (d) line of credit **LO 2-1** 11._____

12. Something of value that can be repossessed if the borrower fails to pay the loan as agreed is called _____. (a) a negotiable instrument (b) a promissory note (c) principal (d) collateral **LO 2-1** 12._____

13. What is a line of credit? (a) a preapproved loan amount that a borrower can access as needed (b) a direct loan of cash made to a consumer at a set interest rate for a specific period of time (c) a legal contract that requires a borrower to make principal payments plus interest (d) a type of loan for which collateral serves as security for payment **LO 2-1** 13._____

14. _____ are for students who have the greatest need and meet rigid eligibility requirements. (a) Subsidized Federal Stafford Loans (b) Federal Perkins Loans (c) Parent PLUS Loans (d) Unsubsidized Federal Stafford Loans **LO 2-1** 14._____

15. Which of these is an example of a *charge card*? (a) a Visa card (b) a Macy's card (c) a Discover card (d) an American Express card **LO 2-1** 15._____

16. With revolving credit, _____. (a) no interest is charged to the user (b) you must pay your   16._____
credit balance in full each month (c) you can keep using your account until you reach your
credit limit or until you close the account (d) all of these **LO 2-1**

17. Which of these is *not* one of the three national credit bureaus? (a) American Express   17._____
(b) TransUnion (c) Experian (d) Equifax **LO 2-2**

18. A statement of your credit history issued by a credit bureau is called a _____. (a) credit   18._____
score (b) credit report (c) balance sheet (d) risk assessment **LO 2-2**

19. FICO scores are calculated on each of the following categories *except*? (a) payment history   19._____
(b) amounts owed (c) personal wealth (d) types of credit used **LO 2-2**

20. To improve your credit score, you should do all of the following *except* _____. (a) pay   20._____
more than the minimum payment (b) reduce your outstanding credit (c) do not apply for more
than one credit card at a time (d) reduce your amount of unused credit **LO 2-2**

Part 3 Short Answer

Directions: Read the following questions, and write your response.

21. Define the term *consumer loan*. **LO 2-1**

22. What is the difference between a credit card and a charge card? **LO 2-1**

23. What is *unused credit*? **LO 2-2**

Part 4 Critical Thinking

Directions: Read the following question, and write your response.

24. What is the advantage of using a charge card rather than a credit card? Which would you prefer to use?
Why? **LO 2-1**

25. Draw a flowchart to illustrate the circular-flow model of problems caused by mismanaging credit.
LO 2-2

10-3 Consumer Debt and Bankruptcy

Part 1 True or False

Directions: Place a *T* for True or an *F* for False in the Answers column to show whether each of the following statements is true or false.

Answers

1. When you begin using credit, you should not use too much at first. **LO 3-1**

   1._____

2. If you are paying on a credit account that has an ongoing balance, the sooner you pay your bill, the less interest you will pay. **LO 3-1**

   2._____

3. It is illegal for credit card companies to solicit new customers by mail. **LO 3-1**

   3._____

4. It is a good idea to use cash to make small purchases such as lunch or a cup of coffee. **LO 3-1**

   4._____

5. One way to avoid credit card fraud is to loan your credit card only to family members and trusted friends. **LO 3-1**

   5._____

6. *Bankruptcy* is a legal procedure to relieve a person of excessive debt. **LO 3-2**

   6._____

7. Chapter 7 bankruptcy is also known as *simple bankruptcy*. **LO 3-2**

   7._____

8. Sometimes, filing bankruptcy is the best economic choice a person can make. **LO 3-2**

   8._____

9. People who declare bankruptcy are not allowed to keep any of their personal property; everything they own is sold to pay off creditors. **LO 3-2**

   9._____

10. If you declare bankruptcy, secured debt will remain even if you claim the debt as exempt. **LO 3-2**

    10._____

Part 2 Multiple Choice

Directions: In the Answers column, write the letter that represents the word, or group of words, that correctly completes the statement or answers the question.

Answers

11. The time period when your credit account is closed to prepare your monthly statement is called the _____. (a) grace period (b) transaction cycle (c) billing cycle (d) closing period **LO 3-1**

    11._____

12. If your credit card account is typical, you will have at least _____ days to pay your account from the bill's closing date. (a) 5 (b) 10 (c) 20 (d) 30 **LO 3-1**

    12._____

13. _____ is a person's outstanding debt obligations at any point in time. (a) Unused credit (b) A credit score (c) Secured debt (d) A debt load **LO 3-1**

    13._____

14. According to the 20/10 rule, your _____ should not exceed 20% of your yearly take-home pay. (a) house payment (b) revolving debt (c) installment debt (d) total debt **LO 3-1**

    14._____

15. This is a type of loan that charges a large upfront fee. (a) secured loan (b) advance-fee loan (c) single-payment loan (d) debt consolidation loan **LO 3-1**

    15._____

16. A(n) _____ is a court order that pardons a debtor from having to pay previous debt obligations. (a) discharge (b) automatic stay (c) injunction (d) petition **LO 3-2**

    16._____

17. Which type of bankruptcy is also known as *business reorganization*? (a) Chapter 13 (b) Chapter 11 (c) Chapter 7 (d) Chapter 3 **LO 3-2**

    17._____

18. Kate is way behind with her bills, but she has a steady job and a good income. She wants to pay off as much of her debt as possible over the next three or four years. The best solution for Kate would probably be to file for _____. (a) liquidation bankruptcy (b) Chapter 7 bankruptcy (c) Chapter 11 bankruptcy (d) Chapter 13 bankruptcy **LO 3-2**   18._____

19. Property that a debtor does not have to forfeit to pay creditors is called _____. (a) security (b) collateral (c) unsecured assets (d) a bankruptcy exemption **LO 3-2**   19._____

20. Bankruptcy stays in your credit file for _____, and you cannot declare bankruptcy again for _____ years. (a) six; ten (b) five; three (c) ten; six (d) three; five **LO 3-2**   20._____

Part 3 Short Answer

Directions: Read the following questions, and write your response.

21. What is a *grace period*? **LO 3-1**

22. Briefly explain how a debt repayment plan works. **LO 3-1**

23. List at least five common reasons why debtors seek bankruptcy. **LO 3-2**

Part 4 Critical Thinking

Directions: Read the following questions, and write your response.

24. When you receive a credit offer, what elements of the offer should you analyze carefully? **LO 3-1**

25. Angela's yearly take-home pay is $40,000. She makes a monthly installment payment to a furniture store $500 each month. Her monthly credit card debt is $250. Analyze Angela's financial situation using the 20/10 rule. **LO 3-1**

Chapter 10 Review

Part 1 True or False

Directions: Place a *T* for True or an *F* for False in the Answers column to show whether each of the following statements is true or false.

Answers

1. Using a credit card to pay for purchases is probably the best way to avoid buying items on impulse. **LO 1-1**
1._____

2. When using credit, people often buy where they have credit available, whether or not they are getting the best price. **LO 1-2**
2._____

3. Interest lowers the cost of your purchases. **LO 1-3**
3._____

4. A promissory note cannot be sold or assigned to another person or company for collection. **LO 2-1**
4._____

5. With most student loans, the student is expected to begin repayment in his or her senior year. **LO 2-1**
5._____

6. The more risk creditors take, the more careful they become in granting credit. **LO 2-2**
6._____

7. Consumer credit counseling services are for-profit organizations that attempt to collect payments for creditors from deadbeat debtors. **LO 3-1**
7._____

8. Do not give credit card information to anyone who contacts you by phone. **LO 3-1**
8._____

9. Chapter 13 bankruptcy is also known as *individual debt adjustment*. **LO 3-2**
9._____

10. It is illegal for a creditor to charge you higher rates if you have filed for bankruptcy. **LO 3-2**
10._____

Part 2 Multiple Choice

Directions: In the Answers column, write the letter that represents the word, or group of words, that correctly completes the statement or answers the question.

Answers

11. The first step of a buying plan is to _____. (a) research your options (b) identify your limits (c) review your options (d) define your goal **LO 1-1**
11._____

12. Using credit _____. (a) makes it less likely that you will shop around for the best deal (b) tends to reduce your standard of living (c) severely limits your financing options (d) all of these **LO 1-2**
12._____

13. A loan that requires collateral is also sometimes called _____. (a) unsecured debt (b) revolving debt (c) secured debt (d) installment debt **LO 2-1**
13._____

14. Which type of business commonly offers service credit? (a) grocery store (b) utility company (c) airline (d) restaurant **LO 2-1**
14._____

15. An excellent FICO score would be in the _____. (a) 500s or below (b) 600s (c) 700s (d) 760–850 range or higher **LO 2-2**
15._____

16. Information about closed accounts is kept in a credit report for _____ years. (a) three (b) five (c) ten (d) twenty **LO 2-2**
16._____

17. The longer the _____, the more time you have to pay before interest is charged. (a) debt load (b) installment period (c) line of credit (d) grace period **LO 3-1**
17._____

18. Equity stripping is _____. (a) offering a large loan that pays off all of a debtor's   18._____
individual, smaller accounts (b) extending a loan to a distressed homeowner who cannot
afford the payments (c) requiring a borrower to put up something of value that can be
repossessed if he or she fails to pay off the loan (d) offering a consumer a loan with a large
up-front fee **LO 3-1**

19. When debtors try to hide assets so they cannot be used to pay off debts, they are _____.   19._____
(a) committing bankruptcy fraud (b) requesting an automatic stay (c) declaring a bankruptcy
exemption (d) discharging the debt **LO 3-2**

20. Which of the following debts would *not* be discharged by bankruptcy? (a) business loans   20._____
(b) automobile loan (c) child support (d) all of these **LO 3-2**

Part 3 Short Answer

Directions: Read the following questions, and write your response.

21. How does using credit give you buying power? **LO 1-2**

22. Identify two purposes of bankruptcy law. **LO 3-2**

Part 4 Critical Thinking

Directions: Read the following question, and write your response.

23. The guidelines for improving credit scores suggest keeping balances owed on accounts less than 50% of
the available credit. For the following accounts, determine if each meets the guidelines. Write *yes* or *no*
next to each account to indicate your answer. **LO 2-2**

Credit limit $5,000, balance of $2,000 _____

Credit limit $1,000, balance of $875   _____

Credit limit $7,500, balance of $4,000 _____

Credit limit $1,800, balance of $700   _____

11-1 Gross Domestic Product

Part 1 True or False

Directions: Place a *T* for True or an *F* for False in the Answers column to show whether each of the following statements is true or false.

Answers

1. Only the market value of tangible goods are included in the calculation of gross domestic product (GDP). **LO 1-1**

    1._____

2. Tom sells a box of old records at a yard sale. The sale of these records would not be included in GDP. **LO 1-1**

    2._____

3. Intermediate goods are purchased for consumption by the ultimate user. **LO 1-1**

    3._____

4. The circular-flow model shows the exchange of money, products, and resources between businesses, households, and government. **LO 1-2**

    4._____

5. The upper half of the circular-flow model represents supply; the bottom half represents demand. **LO 1-2**

    5._____

6. Government spending in the circular-flow model is financed through taxes. **LO 1-2**

    6._____

7. Businesses and households are both buyers and sellers in the circular-flow model. **LO 1-2**

    7._____

8. In the calculation of GDP, *investment* includes purchases by government at the federal, state, and local levels. **LO 1-3**

    8._____

9. *Real GDP* is GDP measured in current prices. **LO 1-3**

    9._____

10. A country's GDP per capita and other quality-of-life indicators generally are related to the country's ranking in economic freedom. **LO 1-3**

    10._____

Part 2 Multiple Choice

Directions: In the Answers column, write the letter that represents the word, or group of words, that correctly completes the statement or answers the question.

Answers

11. Which of the following would *not* be counted in GDP? (a) the amount of money spent to build a new shopping center (b) the value of the work performed by a stay-at-home mother who does the family cooking and cleaning (c) the earnings of a restaurant chef (d) the amount of money people spend on new automobile purchases **LO 1-1**

    11._____

12. What is a *transfer payment*? (a) a government payment to persons not in exchange for goods or services produced (b) an exchange of previously produced goods (c) the exchange of the certificate of ownership in a business (d) economic production that is paid "off the books" **LO 1-1**

    12._____

13. Noah washes his neighbor's car and is paid $25. Noah does not report this income on his tax return. This transaction would be considered _____. (a) a secondhand transaction (b) a transfer payment (c) part of the underground economy (d) a nonmarket activity **LO 1-1**

    13._____

14. Which of these would be considered an intermediate good? (a) an MP3 player purchased by a junior high school student (b) potatoes purchased by a fast-food restaurant (c) a package of printer paper purchased by a dentist's office (d) a haircut at a barber shop **LO 1-1**

    14._____

15. The circular-flow model shows the economic relationships between _____. (a) wages   15._____
and salaries (b) goods and services (c) income and standard of living (d) businesses,
households, and government **LO 1-2**

16. In the circular-flow model, money flows from households to businesses in the _____.   16._____
(a) product markets (b) factor markets (c) resource markets (d) all of these **LO 1-2**

17. In the circular-flow model, money flows in the form of _____ from the resource market to   17._____
households? (a) savings (b) credit (c) interest (d) wages **LO 1-2**

18. Which of the following would be considered a nondurable good? (a) a couch (b) a television   18._____
(c) a carton of milk (d) a wristwatch **LO 1-3**

19. Which of these statements regarding the calculation of GDP is *correct*? (a) Higher exports   19._____
relative to imports increases GDP. (b) Spending for durable goods is much higher than
spending for services. (c) In the formula for GDP, *investment* refers to the purchase of stocks
and bonds. (d) Government spending is not considered in the calculation of GDP. **LO 1-3**

20. GDP divided by the total population is _____. (a) aggregate GDP (b) nominal GDP   20._____
(c) GDP per capita (d) real GDP **LO 1-3**

Part 3 Short Answer

Directions: Read the following questions, and write your response.

21. Why aren't intermediate goods included in a measure of GDP? **LO 1-1**

22. What do businesses and households do in the *product market* of the circular-flow model? What about the
resource market? **LO 1-2**

23. What are the components of GDP? What is the largest of these? **LO 1-3**

Part 4 Critical Thinking

24. In the graphic organizer below, give five examples of a final good and five examples of an intermediate
good. **LO 1-1**

Final Goods	Intermediate Goods

11-2 Business Cycles and Economic Growth

Part 1 True or False

Directions: Place a *T* for True or an *F* for False in the Answers column to show whether each of the following statements is true or false.

Answers

1. Business cycles always exist in market economies. **LO 2-1**   1._____

2. Economists can very accurately predict the phases of the business cycle. **LO 2-1**   2._____

3. A business cycle is divided into three phases: peak, valley, and expansion. **LO 2-1**   3._____

4. A general rule is that a recession is six months in which there is a decline in real GDP.   4._____
   LO 2-1

5. Over time, real GDP tends to rise. **LO 2-1**   5._____

6. Since 2010, the United States has had the largest rate of growth in real GDP of any country   6._____
   in the world. **LO 2-1**

7. Lagging indicators change *after* real GDP changes. **LO 2-1**   7._____

8. Most economists agree that changes in total spending do not greatly affect real GDP.   8._____
   LO 2-2

9. Consumer optimism often can lead to an expansion in the business cycle. **LO 2-2**   9._____

10. A recession is the result of declines in sectors of real GDP. **LO 2-2**   10._____

Part 2 Multiple Choice

Directions: In the Answers column, write the letter that represents the word, or group of words, that correctly completes the statement or answers the question.

Answers

11. A key measure of business cycles is the rise and fall in _____. (a) supply and demand   11._____
    (b) the circular-flow model (c) the production possibilities curve (d) real GDP **LO 2-1**

12. At the _____ stage of the business cycle, the economy is operating near its production   12._____
    possibilities curve. (a) peak (b) plateau (c) valley (d) trough **LO 2-1**

13. A downturn in the business cycle during which real GDP declines is called a _____.   13._____
    (a) trench (b) regression (c) recession (d) trough **LO 2-1**

14. At the trough stage of the business cycle, _____. (a) real GDP reaches its maximum   14._____
    (b) unemployment is at its highest level relative to recent years (c) supply and demand reach
    equilibrium (d) real GDP rises slightly **LO 2-1**

15. An *expansion* _____. (a) can occur at any time in the business cycle (b) follows a trough 15._____
    in the business cycle (c) usually occurs right after the peak in the business cycle (d) is a
    temporary high point in the business cycle **LO 2-1**

16. Economists define the term *economic growth* as _____. (a) a period when an economy is   16._____
    operating exactly at its production possibilities curve (b) an increase in business profits
    relative to the previous year (c) a measurable rise in GDP per capita (d) an increase in a
    nation's real GDP during an expansion **LO 2-1**

17. _____ indicators are economic variables that change before real GDP changes.   17._____
(a) Leading (b) Cumulative (c) Relative (d) Coincident **LO 2-1**

18. Which of these is a lagging indicator? (a) personal income (b) unemployment rate (c) interest   18._____
rates (d) all of these **LO 2-1**

19. Generally speaking, how has real GDP changed in the United States since the 1930s?   19._____
(a) increased (b) decreased (c) remained static (d) short periods of modest increase followed
by extended declines **LO 2-1**

20. A decline in economic growth can be caused by _____. (a) increased business investment   20._____
in plants and equipment (b) an expansion of government spending (c) a decrease in foreign
spending for exports relative to spending for imports (d) all of these **LO 2-2**

Part 3 Short Answer

Directions: Read the following questions, and write your response.

21. Define the term *business cycle*. **LO 2-1**

22. Since 1929, which years had the highest annual real GDP growth in the United States? How do you
explain this? **LO 2-1**

23. How would an economist answer the question: What causes the business cycle? **LO 2-2**

Part 4 Critical Thinking

Directions: Read the following questions, and write your response.

24. In which phase of the business cycle would you place the current U.S. economy? Defend your answer.
LO 2-1

25. What would be the best time in the business cycle for someone to start a new business? **LO 2-1**

26. In the space below, write a headline you might see in the business section of a newspaper during a period
of economic expansion. Then write a headline you might see during a period of recession. Use leading
indicators and/or the components of GDP in your answer. **LO 2-1/LO 2-2**

Chapter 11 Review

Part 1 True or False

Directions: Place a *T* for True or an *F* for False in the Answers column to show whether each of the following statements is true or false.

Answers

1. GDP measures value using the number or amount of raw goods produced, not by using a dollar figure. **LO 1-1**

    1. _____

2. It's a hot summer day, so you buy a cold drink to quench your thirst. Your purchase would be counted in GDP. **LO 1-1**

    2._____

3. In the circular-flow model, households buy goods and services from businesses in resource markets. **LO 1-2**

    3. _____

4. When calculating GDP, only durable goods are factored into consumption. **LO 1-3**

    4._____

5. To determine how prices have changed over the years, you need to know both nominal GDP and real GDP. **LO 1-3**

    5. _____

6. Real GDP provides a more accurate picture of the economy than nominal GDP. **LO 1-3**

    6. _____

7. A recession follows each peak in the business cycle. **LO 2-1**

    7. _____

8. During a recession, an economy is functioning outside its production possibilities curve. **LO 2-1**

    8. _____

9. The government's chief forecasting gauge for business cycles is the index of leading indicators. **LO 2-1**

    9. _____

10. The longest expansion in U.S. history occurred over ten years from 1991 to 2001. **LO 2-1**

    10. _____

Part 2 Multiple Choice

Directions: In the Answers column, write the letter that represents the word, or group of words, that correctly completes the statement or answers the question.

Answers

11. GDP may be defined as _____. (a) the economic value of all resources used in the production of a country's annual output (b) the market value of all final goods and services produced annually in a country (c) all annual income earned by households in a country (d) total spending on factors of production in a given year **LO 1-1**

    11. _____

12. Used goods _____. (a) were counted in GDP in the year when they were newly produced (b) are included in GDP every time they are bought and resold (c) are subtracted from real GDP whenever they are bought and resold (d) are included in GDP only if they are not part of the underground economy **LO 1-1**

    12. _____

13. Which of these is an example of a final good? (a) the chicken you purchase at the grocery store to cook for supper tonight (b) the chicken purchased by a restaurant to prepare for customers tonight (c) both of these (d) neither of these **LO 1-2**

    13. _____

14. In the circular-flow model, households _____. (a) buy products only (b) sell factors of production only (c) sell factors of production *and* buy products (d) buy factors of production *and* sell products **LO 1-2**

    14. _____

15. Which of the following would be accounted for in the product market of the circular-flow model? (a) salaries paid to police officers (b) business spending for office supplies (c) government purchase of military aircraft (d) none of these **LO 1-3**   15. _____

16. It's a hot summer day, so you buy a cold drink to quench your thirst. Your purchase would be considered both a(n) _____ good and a(n) _____ good. (a) final; nondurable (b) intermediate; nondurable (c) final; durable (d) intermediate; durable **LO 1-1/LO 1-3**   16. _____

17. Since the end of World War II, recessions in the United States have averaged _____. (a) 2 months (b) 9 months (c) 11 months (d) 18 months **LO 2-1**   17. _____

18. A 3 percent annual growth in an economy will lead to a doubling of real GDP in about _____. (a) 3 years (b) 9 years (c) 24 years (d) 50 years **LO 2-1**   18. _____

19. An economic expansion is also sometimes referred to as a _____. (a) recovery (b) trough (c) valley (d) plateau **LO 2-1**   19. _____

20. Suppose the value of exports decreases by $50 billion and the value of imports increases by $30 billion. What will result? (a) GDP will increase (b) GDP will decline (c) economic expansion will occur (d) the economy will approach its peak **LO 2-2**   20. _____

Part 3 Short Answer

Directions: Read the following questions, and write your response.

21. Government accountants calculating GDP exclude which five types of transactions? **LO 1-3**

22. Nominal GDP grows in three possible ways. Name them. **LO 1-3**

Part 4 Critical Thinking

Directions: Read the following question, and write your response.

23. For each variable listed below, indicate if it is a leading indicator, a coincident indicator, or a lagging indicator. **LO 2-1**

    Labor cost _____

    Money supply _____

    Unemployment claims _____

    Manufacturing sales _____

    Unemployment rate _____

    Average workweek _____

    Industrial production _____

24. How might a cut in taxes lead to a decline and an increase in economic growth? **LO 2-2**

12-1 Unemployment

Part 1 True or False

Directions: Place a *T* for True or an *F* for False in the Answers column to show whether each of the following statements is true or false.

Answers

1. The unemployment rate is the percentage of all citizens over the age of 16 who are actively seeking work but are not employed. **LO 1-1**

   1._____

2. *Discouraged workers* are persons who want to work but have given up looking for work. **LO 1-1**

   2._____

3. The unemployment rate is calculated by the Bureau of Labor Statistics. **LO 1-1**

   3._____

4. People who are underemployed are not reflected in the government's unemployment rate. **LO 1-1**

   4._____

5. Following the Great Recession of the early 2000s, the unemployment rate reached over 25 percent in 2010. **LO 1-1**

   5._____

6. Frictional, seasonal, and structural unemployment exist even in a strong and growing economy. **LO 1-2**

   6._____

7. Frictional unemployment usually lasts a very long time. **LO 1-2**

   7._____

8. Cyclical unemployment decreases during times of business expansion. **LO 1-2**

   8._____

9. The practice of a company having its work done by another company in another country is called *outsourcing*. **LO 1-2**

   9._____

10. Unemployment rates are higher among college graduates than among those with only a high school education. **LO 1-2**

   10._____

Part 2 Multiple Choice

Directions: In the Answers column, write the letter that represents the word, or group of words, that correctly completes the statement or answers the question.

Answers

11. Which of the following groups is not considered part of the civilian labor force? (a) retirees (b) persons with disabilities (c) persons serving in the Armed Forces (d) all of these **LO 1-1**

   11._____

12. Which of these is an example of *underemployment*? (a) A college graduate is working as a clerk in a bookstore. (b) A seamstress in a garment factory is promoted to supervisor. (c) A high school graduate takes a job selling automobiles. (d) An apprentice plumber finds a job with a plumbing company in another town. **LO 1-1**

   12._____

13. Which of these is a question the BLS asks to determine if a person is unemployed? (a) "Do you like your job?" (b) "How long have you held your current job?" (c) "Have you looked for work in the last month?" (d) "Have you had a job interview in the last six months?" **LO 1-1**

   13._____

14. The official unemployment rate during a recession might actually be underestimated because _____. (a) it does not count students and household workers (b) it does not count discouraged workers (c) people who are working in the underground economy are not counted (d) all of these **LO 1-1**

   14._____

15. In 2010, which of these countries had an unemployment rate *higher* than the United States?   15._____
(a) Greece (b) China (c) Germany (d) Japan **LO 1-1**

16. Tim left his job last month as a computer programmer and is looking for a programming job   16._____
at another software firm. This is an example of _____. (a) underemployment (b) seasonal
unemployment (c) frictional unemployment (d) outsourcing **LO 1-2**

17. Unemployment caused when the skills of workers do not match the skills required for   17._____
existing jobs is _____ unemployment. (a) cyclical (b) aptitude (c) global (d) structural
LO 1-2

18. During a recession we can expect to see an increase in _____. (a) underemployment   18._____
(b) cyclical unemployment (c) frictional unemployment(d) structural unemployment **LO 1-2**

19. When an economy is at full employment, _____. (a) there is no cyclical unemployment   19._____
(b) the unemployment rate is at zero (c) there is no seasonal unemployment (d) all of these
LO 1-2

20. Which of the following statements about unemployment in 2010 is *correct*? (a) The   20._____
unemployment rate for females was greater than for males. (b) The unemployment rate for
African-Americans was higher than that for whites and Hispanics. (c) The unemployment
rate for teenagers was very low. (d) The unemployment rate for college graduates was
relatively high. **LO 1-2**

Part 3 Short Answer

Directions: Read the following questions, and write your response.

21. What is the official definition of the *civilian labor force*? **LO 1-1**

22. Identify four causes of structural unemployment. **LO 1-2**

Part 4 Critical Thinking

Directions: Read the following questions, and write your response.

23. Suppose that 400,000 people are unemployed and there are 4.5 million people in the labor force. What is
the unemployment rate? **LO 1-1**

24. Provide an example of frictional unemployment, structural unemployment, seasonal unemployment, and
cyclical unemployment. **LO 1-2**

12-2 Inflation

Part 1 True or False

Directions: Place a *T* for True or an *F* for False in the Answers column to show whether each of the following statements is true or false.

Answers

1. Rising price levels affect both consumers and producers in a market economy. **LO 2-1**

    1._____

2. When prices are rising rapidly and the nation is experiencing inflation, good consumer decision-making skills are critical. **LO 2-1**

    2._____

3. People on fixed incomes are largely unaffected by rising inflation. **LO 2-1**

    3._____

4. Disinflation often happens when demand for a product is not the same throughout the year. **LO 2-2**

    4._____

5. During the Great Depression, the United States experienced a prolonged period of hyperinflation. **LO 2-2**

    5._____

6. Some products go down in price over time even when the market as a whole is not experiencing a period of deflation. **LO 2-2**

    6._____

7. Economists agree that there is only one root cause of inflation. **LO 2-3**

    7._____

8. The most common form of inflation is cost-push inflation. **LO 2-3**

    8._____

9. Economists agree that there is a direct relationship between inflation and employment. **LO 2-3**

    9._____

10. Over the past 20 years, the United States has experienced relatively low inflation rates. **LO 2-3**

    10._____

Part 2 Multiple Choice

Directions: In the Answers column, write the letter that represents the word, or group of words, that correctly completes the statement or answers the question.

Answers

11. A pay increase from employers that is intended to offset the effects of inflation is called a(n) _____. B (a) income correction (b) salary augmentation (c) cost-of-living adjustment (d) price index adjustment **LO 2-1**

    11._____

12. The Consumer Price Index measures _____. (a) the cost of major consumer goods such as autos and appliances over time (b) the cost of a "market basket" of consumer goods and services on a specific day (c) the cost of all consumer goods and services sold in an economy in one year (d) the cost of a "market basket" of consumer goods and services over time **LO 2-1**

    12._____

13. Suppose the annual inflation rate is 7 percent, and you have an investment that is paying 4 percent interest. Which of the following would be the best action for you to take? (a) Leave your money where it is. (b) Reinvest your money to earn more than 7 percent interest. (c) Withdraw your money and put it under your mattress. (d) Move your money to an investment that is earning at least 5 percent interest. **LO 2-1**

    13._____

14. When prices are rising but the rate of increase is slowing, the economy is in a period of _____. (a) disinflation (b) stagflation (c) hyperinflation (d) deflation **LO 2-2**

    14._____

15. Many economists consider inflation rates of _____ percent or higher to be hyperinflation. (a) 20 (b) 30 (c) 40 (d) 50 **LO 2-2**   15._____

16. This is the opposite of inflation. (a) metaflation (b) hyperinflation (c) deflation (d) stagflation **LO 2-2**   16._____

17. Consumers want to buy more goods and services than producers are willing or able to supply. This will likely lead to _____. (a) demand-pull inflation (b) stagflation (c) metaflation (d) real-cost inflation **LO 2-3**   17._____

18. Which of the following will especially benefit a business during times of cost-push inflation? (a) price gouging (b) high productivity (c) a COLA (d) the wage-price spiral **LO 2-3**   18._____

19. As the world's supply of oil begins to become depleted, the likelihood of _____ becomes greater. (a) stagflation (b) demand-pull inflation (c) deflation (d) real-cost inflation **LO 2-3**   19._____

20. During a period of high inflation, which of the following is probably the best investment? (a) stocks (b) a fixed-rate savings account (c) a certificate of deposit (d) a checking account **LO 2-3**   20._____

Part 3 Short Answer

Directions: Read the following questions, and write your response.

21. Provide a brief definition for the term *inflation*. What happens to the value of the dollar during periods of increasing inflation? **LO 2-1**

22. What is deflation and why does it occur? **LO 2-2**

Part 4 Critical Thinking

Directions: Read the following questions, and write your response.

23. How does demand-pull inflation affect the unemployment rate? How does cost-push inflation affect it? Explain your answers. **LO 2-3**

Chapter 12 Review

Part 1 True or False

Directions: Place a *T* for True or an *F* for False in the Answers column to show whether each of the following statements is true or false.

Answers

1. Retirees are not considered part of the labor force. **LO 1-1**   1._____

2. Since 1929, the lowest unemployment rate in the United States was achieved in 2010. **LO 1-1**   2._____

3. Structurally unemployed workers are usually without work for only a short time. **LO 1-2**   3._____

4. Various labor market groups share the impact of unemployment unequally. **LO 1-2**   4._____

5. A cost-of-living adjustment provides more spending power to consumers. **LO 2-1**   5._____

6. Raising prices to meet the impact of inflation gives a business more spending power. **LO 2-1**   6._____

7. Inflation affects pricing as well as purchasing decisions. **LO 2-2**   7._____

8. Deflation is usually a good sign for an economy because prices for consumer goods and services are going down. **LO 2-2**   8._____

9. Cost-push inflation occurs when producers raise prices because their costs to create products are rising. **LO 2-3**   9._____

10. Inflationary times are the best times for investing. **LO 2-3**   10._____

Part 2 Multiple Choice

Directions: In the Answers column, write the letter that represents the word, or group of words, that correctly completes the statement or answers the question.

Answers

11. Nancy has been looking for a job for more than one year, but she has finally given up her search. She wants to work, but she just can't seem to find anything. The Bureau of Labor Statistics would consider Nancy to be _____. (a) a disgruntled worker (b) outsourced (c) underemployed (d) a discouraged worker **LO 1-1**   11._____

12. During the Great Depression, the unemployment rate in the United States reached as high as _____. (a) 10 percent (b) 15 percent (c) 25 percent (d) 40 percent **LO 1-1**   12._____

13. The cause of frictional unemployment is _____. (a) a sluggish economy (b) a "mismatch" of worker skills with available jobs (c) the transition time to match a job applicant with a job vacancy (d) changes in the seasons **LO 1-2**   13._____

14. Most economists would agree that an unemployment rate of about 5 percent constitutes (a) frictional unemployment (b) full employment (c) underemployment (d) cyclical unemployment **LO 1-2**   14._____

15. One year ago, the CPI was 178. Today it is 185. What is the annual rate of inflation? (a) 3.93% (b) 7% (c) 10.93% (d) 96.21% **LO 2-1**   15._____

16. Of the following, who is likely to benefit from inflation? (a) businesses that have money to lend (b) individuals on fixed incomes (c) employees who do not receive a COLA (d) consumers who depend on credit **LO 2-1**   16._____

17. What is likely to occur with the price of snow shovels in July? (a) hyperinflation   17._____
    (b) stagflation (c) demand-pull inflation (d) disinflation **LO 2-2**

18. During periods of hyperinflation, _____. (a) people tend to save money at very high rates   18._____
    (b) demand for goods and services is sluggish (c) consumers spend their money as fast as
    they can (d) none of these **LO 2-2**

19. Which of the following scenarios is most likely to produce cost-push inflation? (a) wage rates   19._____
    rise steadily and productivity remains the same (b) wage rates rise steadily and productivity
    increases (c) wage rates fall slightly and productivity increases (d) consumer demand is far
    greater than supply **LO 2-3**

20. As resources become scarce or more difficult to obtain, prices rise in the form of _____.   20._____
    (a) cost-push inflation (b) demand-pull inflation (c) real-cost inflation (d) hyperinflation
    LO 2-3

Part 3 Short Answer

Directions: Read the following questions, and write your response.

21. Define the term *underemployed person*. Give an example of an underemployed person. **LO 1-1**

22. Compare the unemployment rates for American teenagers as of 2010 with other American workers. What
    accounts for the difference? **LO 1-2**

Part 4 Critical Thinking

Directions: Read the following questions, and write your response.

23. Suppose the inflation rate is 15 percent. How would you predict that this would affect saving and
    investing? What might be the impact on the availability of business loans? **LO 2-2**

24. Sal and Janice have a large, fixed-rate mortgage. The interest rate on the mortgage is 4.75 percent.
    Suppose the annual inflation rate in recent years has been close to 8 percent. Would this high inflation
    rate benefit or hurt Sal and Janice? Explain. **LO 2-1**

13-1 Fiscal Policy

Part 1 True or False

Directions: Place a *T* for True or an *F* for False in the Answers column to show whether each of the following statements is true or false.

Answers

1. Fiscal policy is the use of federal government spending and taxes to achieve economic goals. **LO 1-1** 1._____

2. During a recession the government may use contractionary fiscal policy. **LO 1-1** 2._____

3. Macroeconomic equilibrium is the price level where the aggregate demand curve intersects the aggregate supply curve. **LO 1-1** 3._____

4. Either increasing government spending or cutting taxes shifts the aggregate demand curve rightward. **LO 1-1** 4._____

5. Contractionary fiscal policy increases real GDP; it also reduces unemployment. **LO 1-1** 5._____

6. Before the 1930s, fiscal policy was rarely used to influence the U.S. economy. **LO 1-2** 6._____

7. Keynes believed that fiscal policy should be used only in times of low unemployment. **LO 1-2** 7._____

8. After his election in 1932, Franklin D. Roosevelt used contractionary fiscal policy to try to restore the economy. **LO 1-2** 8._____

9. According to economist Arthur Laffer, as the tax rate climbs, total tax collections decrease because there is less incentive for people to work, save, invest, and produce. **LO 1-2** 9._____

10. Most economists accept the basic idea behind the Laffer curve. **LO 1-2** 10._____

Part 2 Multiple Choice

Directions: In the Answers column, write the letter that represents the word, or group of words, that correctly completes the statement or answers the question.

Answers

11. The government uses fiscal policy to try achieve _____. (a) full employment (b) stable prices (c) economic growth (d) all of these **LO 1-1** 11._____

12. Expansionary fiscal policy _____. (a) increases federal government spending (b) increases taxes (c) is used to decrease real GDP (d) is most likely to be used during a time of rising prices **LO 1-1** 12._____

13. Real gross domestic product that will be produced at different price levels is shown on the _____. (a) cumulative supply curve (b) aggregate demand curve (c) aggregate supply curve (d) cumulative demand curve **LO 1-1** 13._____

14. If the price level is above the level of macroeconomic equilibrium, then _____. (a) the shortage of products forces businesses to raise their prices (b) the real GDP supplied is greater than real GDP purchased (c) businesses respond by producing more goods and services (d) real GDP demanded exceeds real GDP supplied **LO 1-1** 14._____

15. Contractionary fiscal policy will cause the aggregate demand curve to _____. (a) shift to the right (b) shift to the left (c) remain unchanged (d) change from downward-sloping to upward-sloping **LO 1-1** 15._____

16. An increase in aggregate demand would result in _____. (a) an increase in real GDP   16._____
(b) a rise in unemployment (c) a drop in the price of goods and services (d) all of these **LO 1-1**

17. Keynesian economic theory was prompted by _____. (a) the Civil War (b) World War I   17._____
(c) the Great Depression (d) the Korean War **LO 1-2**

18. A classical economist would most likely agree that _____. (a) the source of unemployment   18._____
lies within the market system (b) free market forces cannot reduce unemployment
(c) government should not interfere in the marketplace (d) a free market is self-regulating
LO 1-2

19. The Laffer curve shows _____. (a) the relationship between tax rates and total tax revenues   19._____
(b) how supply influences demand (c) that contractionary fiscal policy will have no effect on
the aggregate demand curve (d) that expansionary fiscal policy and unemployment have a
positive relationship **LO 1-2**

20. Suppose the federal income tax rate is 70 percent. If the rate is reduced to 50 percent, Arthur   20._____
Laffer would predict that _____. (a) tax revenues would decrease (b) tax revenues would
increase (c) people would increase their attempts to avoid paying taxes (d) economic activity
would decline **LO 1-2**

Part 3 Short Answer

Directions: Read the following questions, and write your response.

21. Name the two basic fiscal policies the federal government uses depending on the condition of the
economy, and identify when each policy would be used. **LO 1-1**

22. Which economist can be called the "Father of Classical Economics"? **LO 1-2**

Part 4 Critical Thinking

Directions: Read the following questions, and write your response.

23. What did Keynes mean by his remark, "In the long run we are all dead"? Why does this lead to the
conclusion that government should intervene during times of high unemployment? **LO 1-2**

13-2 Government Budgets and Types of Taxes

Part 1 True or False

Directions: Place a *T* for True or an *F* for False in the Answers column to show whether each of the following statements is true or false.

Answers

1. Programs such as Social Security, Medicare, and unemployment compensation make up only a small fraction of the federal budget. **LO 2-1**

1._____

2. Priorities for government spending at the federal level are far different from priorities for government spending at the state and local level. **LO 2-1**

2._____

3. The Sixteenth Amendment to the Constitution gives the federal government the authority to impose an income tax. **LO 2-1**

3._____

4. Businesses are prohibited by law from passing the cost of excise taxes on to consumers. **LO 2-1**

4._____

5. Sales taxes are much more important sources of revenue for the federal government than they are for state and local governments. **LO 2-1**

5._____

6. Much government spending is supported by borrowing rather than by current tax receipts. **LO 2-1**

6._____

7. Individual and corporate income tax rates are progressive. **LO 2-2**

7._____

8. Regressive taxes follow the concept that those who have higher incomes can afford to pay higher tax rates. **LO 2-2**

8._____

9. For individual income tax purposes, there are two ranges of income—or tax brackets—in the United States. **LO 2-2**

9._____

10. There is no perfect example of a flat tax in the United States. **LO 2-2**

10._____

Part 2 Multiple Choice

Directions: In the Answers column, write the letter that represents the word, or group of words, that correctly completes the statement or answers the question.

Answers

11. Since 1950, total government spending grew to about _____ of GDP beginning in 1975. (a) one-tenth (b) one-fourth (c) one-third (d) one-half **LO 2-1**

11._____

12. What are the three largest categories of *federal* government spending? (a) education and health, national defense, veterans' benefits (b) income security, national defense, education and health (c) national defense, education and health, international affairs (d) income security, interest on the federal debt, national defense **LO 2-1**

12._____

13. By far, the largest priority in state and local government budgets is _____. (a) education (b) public welfare (c) health and hospitals (d) highways **LO 2-1**

13._____

14. The largest revenue source for the federal government in 2010 was _____. (a) sales taxes (b) individual income taxes (c) corporate income taxes (d) property taxes **LO 2-1**

14._____

15. This is a tax on the purchase of a specific good or service that is paid by the producer or retailer. (a) property tax (b) tariff (c) sales tax (d) excise tax **LO 2-1**

15._____

16. Total government taxes climbed to their highest level of 34 percent in _____. (a) 1929   16._____
    (b) 1945 (c) 2000 (d) 2010 **LO 2-1**

17. This type of tax charges a higher percentage as income rises. (a) progressive (b) sales   17._____
    (c) property (d) regressive **LO 2-2**

18. Which of these is an example of a regressive tax? (a) sales taxes (b) excise taxes (c) property   18._____
    taxes (d) all of these **LO 2-2**

19. With a flat tax, _____. (a) the tax rate rises as income rises (b) the amount of the tax   19._____
    generally becomes part of the price paid by consumers (c) the tax rate remains the same as
    income rises (d) the tax rate falls as income rises **LO 2-2**

20. Suppose a new tax requires all Americans to pay 2 percent of their income to support public   20._____
    education. What type of taxation would this be? (a) proportional (b) excise (c) regressive
    (d) progressive **LO 2-2**

Part 3 Short Answer

Directions: Read the following questions, and write your response.

21. What types of government programs fall under the category of *income security*? **LO 2-1**

22. What is a *tax base*? Give at least three examples of tax bases. **LO 2-2**

Part 4 Critical Thinking

Directions: Read the following questions, and write your response.

23. Regressive taxes are sometimes said to favor the wealthy. Explain. **LO 2-2**

24. Discuss some possible advantages and disadvantages of adopting a proportional tax system for the federal
    income tax. **LO 2-2**

13-3 Budget Deficits and the National Debt

Part 1 True or False

Directions: Place a *T* for True or an *F* for False in the Answers column to show whether each of the following statements is true or false.

Answers

1. The first step in the federal budgetary process is that Congress submits the budget to the president. **LO 3-1**

   1. _____

2. The Congressional Budget Office advises Congress on the federal budget. **LO 3-1**

   2. _____

3. By February of each year, Congress approves an overall budget outline. **LO 3-1**

   3. _____

4. The budget resolution guides the spending and revenue decisions of the congressional committees that prepare specific spending and tax law bills. **LO 3-1**

   4. _____

5. Between 1998 and 2001, budget surpluses existed. **LO 3-1**

   5. _____

6. As a share of GDP, Franklin Roosevelt's New Deal budget deficits were the largest the United States has ever seen. **LO 3-1**

   6. _____

7. If you own a U.S. government savings bond, you have loaned your funds to the federal government. **LO 3-1**

   7. _____

8. The stock of U.S. Treasury T-bills, notes, and bonds outstanding is the *national debt*. **LO 3-2**

   8. _____

9. Debt must be judged relative to the debtor's ability to repay the principal and interest on the debt. **LO 3-2**

   9. _____

10. Measured as a percentage of GDP, the U.S. national debt is higher today than at any point in history. **LO 3-2**

    10. _____

Part 2 Multiple Choice

Directions: In the Answers column, write the letter that represents the word, or group of words, that correctly completes the statement or answers the question.

Answers

11. Which of the following must occur by the first Monday in February each year? (a) Congress must approve the budget resolution (b) all taxpayers must complete their tax returns (c) the president must submit a budget to Congress (d) the president must sign the budget **LO 3-1**

    11. _____

12. Federal budget committee hearings are held in _____. (a) the House of Representatives (b) the Senate (c) both a and b (d) neither a nor b **LO 3-1**

    12. _____

13. The federal budget outline approved by Congress is called the _____. (a) budget resolution (b) federal deficit (c) revenue bill (d) executive summary **LO 3-1**

    13. _____

14. Suppose government spending totals $50 trillion and tax revenues total $48 trillion. This would be an example of a _____. (a) budget surplus (b) budget deficit (c) bankrupted government (d) balanced budget **LO 3-1**

    14. _____

15. The last year the U.S. government had a budget surplus was _____. (a) 1998 (b) 2001 (c) 2010 (d) none of these; the U.S government has never had a budget surplus **LO 3-1**

    15. _____

16. This occurs when government spending equals tax revenues. (a) budget deficit (b) budget surplus (c) budgetary equilibrium (d) balanced budget **LO 3-1**

    16. _____

17. This is a security that the federal government repays between one to ten years. (a) treasury note (b) T bill (c) treasury bond (d) treasury bill **LO 3-1**   17. _____

18. Government securities such as savings bonds _____. (a) can be purchased only by U.S. citizens (b) are IOUs of the federal government (c) are issued by the Federal Reserve (d) all of these **LO 3-1**   18. _____

19. The national debt crossed the $1 trillion mark in _____. (a) 1919 (b) 1945 (c) 1982 (d) 2010 **LO 3-2**   19. _____

20. Which of the following would contribute to the rising national debt? (a) recession (b) war (c) widespread unemployment (d) all of these **LO 3-2**   20. _____

Part 3 Short Answer

Directions: Read the following questions, and write your response.

21. List the major steps in the federal budgetary process. **LO 3-1**

22. What happens when the government spends more than it collects in taxes? How does the government fund budget deficits? **LO 3-1**

23. Distinguish between treasury bills, treasury notes, and treasury bonds. **LO 3-1**

Part 4 Critical Thinking

Directions: Read the following questions, and write your response.

24. Why might a Keynesian economist oppose a law requiring the federal government to have a balanced budget? **LO 3-1**

25. Should you be concerned about the increasing national debt? Explain your answer. **LO 3-2**

Chapter 13 Review

Part 1 True or False

Directions: Place a *T* for True or an *F* for False in the Answers column to show whether each of the following statements is true or false.

Answers

1. The aggregate demand curve shows real GDP that will be purchased at different price levels. **LO 1-1**

    1. _____

2. Keynes believed that the economy was self-regulating and not in need of government intervention. **LO 1-2**

    2. _____

3. During the Great Depression, Franklin Roosevelt used the principles of classical economics to help create jobs using public works projects. **LO 1-2**

    3. _____

4. The largest spending category for the federal government is education. **LO 2-1**

    4. _____

5. Social insurance taxes are not a significant source of revenue for state and local governments. **LO 2-1**

    5. _____

6. Economists classify all taxes into three types of taxation: income, sales, and property. **LO 2-2**

    6. _____

7. With a proportional tax, everyone pays the same *percentage* of income regardless of the *size* of income. **LO 2-2**

    7. _____

8. The United States has never experienced a budget surplus. **LO 3-1**

    8. _____

9. In 2010, foreigners owned almost one-third of the total national debt. **LO 3-1**

    9. _____

10. The national debt is the accumulation of federal deficits over time. **LO 3-2**

    10. _____

Part 2 Multiple Choice

Directions: In the Answers column, write the letter that represents the word, or group of words, that correctly completes the statement or answers the question.

Answers

11. Expansionary fiscal policy _____ government spending and _____ taxes.
    (a) decreases; increases (b) increases; decreases (c) decreases; decreases (d) increases; increases **LO 1-1**

    11. _____

12. In times of inflation _____. (a) expansionary fiscal policy would likely be employed (b) the goal of fiscal policy would be to slow the growth rate (c) the government would probably increase spending (d) none of these **LO 1-1**

    12. _____

13. Keynesian economics is also called _____. (a) tight-money policy (b) supply-side economics (c) demand-side economics (d) easy-money policy **LO 1-2**

    13. _____

14. This classical economist wrote *The Wealth of Nations*. (a) Adam Smith (b) Arthur Laffer (c) John Maynard Keynes (d) Milton Friedman **LO 1-2**

    14. _____

15. What are the three largest categories of *state and local government* spending? (a) education and health, civilian safety, veterans' benefits (b) income security, national defense, education and health (c) education, public welfare, civilian safety (d) highways, education, health and hospitals **LO 2-1**

    15. _____

16. This category of federal revenue pays for workers' compensation and unemployment insurance. (a) social insurance taxes (b) individual income taxes (c) excise taxes (d) corporate income taxes **LO 2-1**

16._____

17. In 2010, the highest federal income tax was _____. (a) 25 percent (b) 35 percent (c) 50 percent (d) 75 percent **LO 2-2**

17._____

18. A treasury bond is a security that the federal government repays _____. (a) within 30 days (b) in one year or less (c) between one to ten years (d) between 20 to 30 years **LO 3-1**

18._____

19. In 2010, the federal budget deficit was about _____ percent of GDP. (a) 2.4 (b) 5 (c) 10 (d) 15.3 **LO 3-1**

19._____

20. Which foreign country holds the largest percentage of total U.S. national debt? (a) Japan (b) Mexico (c) Canada (d) China **LO 3-1**

20._____

Part 3 Short Answer

Directions: Read the following questions, and write your response.

21. Contrast the views of classical economists with those of Keynesian economists. **LO 1-2**

22. Are property taxes usually considered to be progressive or regressive? Explain. **LO 2-2**

Part 4 Critical Thinking

Directions: Read the following question, and write your response.

23. Under what circumstances might it be desirable for a government to run a budget deficit? Explain your answer. **LO 3-1**

14-1 Federal Reserve System

Part 1 True or False

Directions: Place a *T* for True or an *F* for False in the Answers column to show whether each of the following statements is true or false.

Answers

1. The Federal Reserve is an independent agency of the U.S. government, and its independence is guaranteed by the U.S. Constitution. **LO 1-1**
   1._____

2. The Federal Open Market Committee and the Federal Advisory Council assist the Federal Reserve System's Board of Governors. **LO 1-1**
   2._____

3. The Federal Reserve System is funded by the U.S. Congress. **LO 1-1**
   3._____

4. Nonmember depository institutions are not official members of the Fed team. **LO 1-1**
   4._____

5. The typical bank customer never enters the doors of a Federal Reserve district bank. **LO 1-2**
   5._____

6. The primary role of the Fed is to control the nation's money supply. **LO 1-2**
   6._____

7. Congress created the Federal Deposit Insurance Corporation (FDIC) in response to The Panic of 1907. **LO 1-2**
   7._____

8. The Federal Reserve prints all U.S. currency. **LO 1-2**
   8._____

9. The goal of the Consumer Financial Protection Bureau is to make it easier for consumers to sue banks that deny them loans. **LO 1-2**
   9._____

10. The Fed acts as the lender of last resort to prevent a banking crisis. **LO 1-2**
    10._____

Part 2 Multiple Choice

Directions: In the Answers column, write the letter that represents the word, or group of words, that correctly completes the statement or answers the question.

Answers

11. Who is responsible for overseeing the Fed? (a) the President (b) Congress (c) a panel of governors from the ten largest U.S. states (d) the Supreme Court **LO 1-1**
    11._____

12. There are _____ Federal Reserve Districts and _____ Federal Reserve branch banks located throughout the United States. (a) 12; 25 (b) 25; 12 (c) 7; 12 (d) 7; 25 **LO 1-1**
    12._____

13. This seven-member group supervises the banking system of the United States. (a) Federal Advisory Council (b) Federal Open Market Committee (c) Board of Governors (d) Federal Reserve district bank presidents **LO 1-1**
    13._____

14. The Fed gets funds to operate from _____. (a) the Federal Advisory Council (b) interest income from government securities it holds (c) the U.S. Congress (d) all of these **LO 1-1**
    14._____

15. The Federal Open Market Committee _____. (a) consists of bankers selected from each Federal Reserve District (b) approves loans to banks that pay the Fed interest (c) oversees all nonmember depository institutions that are not Fed member banks (d) directs the buying and selling of U.S. government securities by the Fed **LO 1-1**
    15._____

16. About _____ percent of state-chartered banks are Fed members. (a) 20 (b) 40 (c) 75 (d) none of these; state-chartered banks cannot join the Federal Reserve **LO 1-1**
    16._____

17. This Federal Reserve service collects funds from a check writer's bank and transfers them to the recipient's bank. (a) check kiting (b) overseeing NSF accounts (c) check clearing (d) electronic banking **LO 1-2**

17._____

18. In 2008, the FDIC raised coverage of bank deposits to _____ per customer. (a) $25,000 (b) $100,000 (c) $250,000 (d) $500,000 **LO 1-2**

18._____

19. Which of these is *not* a function of the Fed? (a) offering consumer savings accounts (b) supervising and regulating banks (c) maintaining and circulating currency (d) maintaining federal government checking accounts and gold **LO 1-2**

19._____

20. This law prohibits discrimination based on race, color, gender, marital status, religion, or national origin in the extension of credit. (a) Civil Rights Act (b) Consumer Financial Protection Act (c) Fair Credit Reporting Act (d) Equal Credit Opportunity Act **LO 1-2**

20._____

Part 3 Short Answer

Directions: Read the following questions, and write your response.

21. Explain how the Fed's structure is the result of a compromise between opposing viewpoints of how a central bank should be organized. **LO 1-1**

22. Briefly summarize the check clearing process. **LO 1-2**

Part 4 Critical Thinking

Directions: Read the following question, and write your response.

23. How is the Board of Governors protected from influence by the president or Congress? **LO 1-1**

14-2 Monetary Policy

Part 1 True or False

Directions: Place a *T* for True or an *F* for False in the Answers column to show whether each of the following statements is true or false.

Answers

1. *Monetary policy* is the Federal Reserve's use of changes in the money supply to achieve economic goals. **LO 2-1**

    1._____

2. A lower interest rate increases real GDP and reduces unemployment. **LO 2-1**

    2._____

3. When the economy is experiencing inflation, the Fed would likely favor a contractionary monetary policy. **LO 2-1**

    3._____

4. Contractionary monetary policy results in increased aggregate demand. **LO 2-1**

    4._____

5. The buying and selling of government securities to affect the money supply is called *the law of supply and demand*. **LO 2-1**

    5._____

6. Open market sales generally occur in times of inflation. **LO 2-1**

    6._____

7. The federal funds rate never changes. **LO 2-1**

    7._____

8. The least-used monetary policy tool is changing the reserve requirement. **LO 2-1**

    8._____

9. A decrease in the money supply and higher interest rates shifts the aggregate demand curve rightward. **LO 2-2**

    9._____

10. During the Great Recession of 2007, the Fed used contractionary monetary policy. **LO 2-2**

    10._____

Part 2 Multiple Choice

Directions: In the Answers column, write the letter that represents the word, or group of words, that correctly completes the statement or answers the question.

Answers

11. Which of the following effects is contractionary monetary policy most likely to have? (a) increased real GDP (b) increased unemployment (c) increased consumer spending (d) all of these **LO 2-1**

    11._____

12. During a recession, the Fed may use _____. (a) a tight-money policy (b) a decrease in the money supply (c) expansionary monetary policy (d) contractionary monetary policy **LO 2-1**

    12._____

13. The most important and most-used monetary policy tool is _____. (a) open market operations (b) changing the reserve requirement (c) changing the discount rate (d) increasing the federal funds rate **LO 2-1**

    13._____

14. The open market operation can _____. (a) purchase U.S. government securities (b) sell U.S. government securities (c) both purchase and sell U.S. government securities (d) neither purchase nor sell U.S. government securities **LO 2-1**

    14._____

15. A discount rate increase _____. (a) is an example of contractionary monetary policy (b) is likely to occur in times of recession (c) increases the money supply (d) reduces the cost of borrowing reserves **LO 2-1**

    15._____

16. The *federal funds rate* is the interest rate _____. (a) the Fed charges on loans of reserves to banks (b) mandated by the U.S. Congress for all consumer loans (c) the Fed charges to its best business customers (d) one bank charges another for overnight loans of reserves **LO 2-1**

    16._____

17. Which of the following is true of an expansionary monetary policy? (a) required reserve ratio decreases (b) open market operations purchase (c) money multiplier increases (d) all of these **LO 2-1**   17._____

18. The Fed can increase the required reserve ratio _____. (a) to increase the money supply (b) to make loans harder to obtain (c) to give banks more excess reserves to lend (d) to boost aggregate demand and economic recovery **LO 2-1**   18._____

19. Expansionary monetary policy will cause the aggregate demand curve to _____. (a) shift to the right (b) shift to the left (c) remain unchanged (d) change from downward-sloping to upward-sloping **LO 2-2**   19._____

20. Which of the following policies did the Fed take during the Great Recession of 2007? (a) used open market sales to decrease the money supply (b) increased the reserve requirement (c) dropped the federal funds rate to almost zero percent (d) all of these **LO 2-2**   20._____

Part 3 Short Answer

Directions: Read the following questions, and write your response.

21. Contrast expansionary monetary policy with contractionary monetary policy. **LO 2-1**

22. What is the discount rate? **LO 2-1**

Part 4 Critical Thinking

Directions: Read the following questions, and write your response.

23. Based on the current state of the U.S. economy, do you think the Fed should pursue expansionary or contractionary monetary policy? Explain. **LO 2-1**

24. Does the aggregate demand curve shown below reflect expansionary or contractionary monetary policy? **LO 2-2**

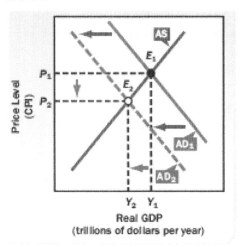

Chapter 14 Federal Reserve and Monetary Policy

Chapter 14 Review

Part 1 True or False

Directions: Place a *T* for True or an *F* for False in the Answers column to show whether each of the following statements is true or false.

Answers

1. The U.S. is the only nation in the world to have separate regional banks instead of a single central bank. **LO 1-1**

   1. _____

2. The Board of Governors does not take orders from the president or legislators. **LO 1-1**

   2. _____

3. About 70 percent of American banks are members of the Fed. **LO 1-1**

   3. _____

4. It is fair to say that the Federal Reserve serves as a "banker's bank." **LO 1-2**

   4. _____

5. The Equal Credit Opportunity Act ensures that everyone who applies for a bank loan will be approved. **LO 1-2**

   5. _____

6. In times of recession, the Fed would pursue policies that would increase consumption spending. **LO 2-1**

   6. _____

7. Open market purchases decrease the amount of reserves that banks have on hand to make new loans. **LO 2-1**

   7. _____

8. Reserves borrowed in the federal funds market have a dramatic effect on the money supply. **LO 2-1**

   8. _____

9. In times of inflation, the required reserve ratio would likely be increased. **LO 2-1**

   9. _____

10. Lower interest rates encourage consumers to borrow and spend more and businesses to increase their investment spending. **LO 2-2**

    10. _____

Part 2 Multiple Choice

Directions: In the Answers column, write the letter that represents the word, or group of words, that correctly completes the statement or answers the question.

Answers

11. Each member of the Board of Governors of the Federal Reserve System serves _____. (a) for 7 years (b) for 14 years (c) until age 65 (d) for life **LO 1-1**

    11. _____

12. This principal spokesperson for the Fed has considerable power over the Fed's policy decisions. (a) the U.S. president (b) chairman of the Board of Governors (c) chairman of the Federal Open Market Committee (d) speaker of the House **LO 1-1**

    12. _____

13. Policy statements known as *directives* are issued by the _____. (a) Board of Governors (b) Regional Federal Reserve Banks (c) Federal Open Market Committee (d) Federal Advisory Council **LO 1-1**

    13. _____

14. Judging from its name, which of the following financial institutions likely is a member of the Fed? (a) Charter One Bank (b) First National Bank (c) Greater Pittsburgh Credit Union (d) Warsaw Savings and Loan **LO 1-1**

    14. _____

15. The FDIC is a government agency that _____. (a) prints all Federal Reserve notes (b) clears all checks that pass through the U.S. banking system (c) insures customer bank deposits up to a predetermined limit if a bank fails (d) resolves consumer complaints against banks **LO 1-2**

    15. _____

16. One of the largest accumulations of gold in the world can be found at the _____ Federal   16. ____
Reserve District Bank. (a) Philadelphia (b) Fort Knox (c) San Francisco (d) New York
LO 1-2

17. Expansionary monetary policy is also sometimes referred to as a(n) _____. (a) free-lunch   17. ____
policy (b) tight-money policy (c) golden-egg policy (d) easy-money policy **LO 2-1**

18. The Fed's purchase of a U.S. treasury bond is an example of _____. (a) a change in the   18. ____
reserve requirement (b) contractionary monetary policy (c) open market operations
(d) none of these **LO 2-1**

19. The _____ market is a private market in which banks lend reserves to each other for less   19. ____
than 24 hours. (a) federal funds (b) open (c) discount (d) expansionary **LO 2-1**

20. A decrease in the money supply will _____. (a) increase real GDP (b) reduce   20. ____
unemployment (c) shift the aggregate demand curve left (d) all of these **LO 2-2**

Part 3 Short Answer

Directions: Read the following questions, and write your response.

21. When was the Federal Reserve created? What event caused Congress to bring the Fed into existence?
LO 1-1

22. When would the Fed likely sell government securities: during a time of recession or inflation? Why?
LO 2-1

Part 4 Critical Thinking

Directions: Read the following question, and write your response.

23. Suppose the Fed wants to expand the money supply. How might it achieve this? **LO 2-1**

15-1 Why Nations Trade

Part 1 True or False

Directions: Place a *T* for True or an *F* for False in the Answers column to show whether each of the following statements is true or false.

Answers

1. World trade is important because it give consumers more choices. **LO 1-1**   1._____

2. All exports of one nation are also imports of other nations. **LO 1-1**   2._____

3. China is the world's largest importer. **LO 1-1**   3._____

4. Only large businesses can import and export goods. **LO 1-1**   4._____

5. Exports are becoming less and less important for the United States. **LO 1-1**   5._____

6. *Comparative advantage* is the ability of a country to produce a good at a lower opportunity cost than another country. **LO 1-2**   6._____

7. According to the theory of absolute advantage, countries should specialize in producing the products they make more efficiently than other countries and trade with other nations for products that they do not make as well. **LO 1-2**   7._____

8. Countries export what they can produce at a lower opportunity cost. **LO 1-2**   8._____

9. If a country is self-sufficient it should not need to participate in international trade. **LO 1-2**   9._____

10. To determine specialization, each country must consider its production possibilities. **LO 1-2**   10._____

Part 2 Multiple Choice

Directions: In the Answers column, write the letter that represents the word, or group of words, that correctly completes the statement or answers the question.

Answers

11. A box of chocolates that is produced in Belgium and sold in the United States has been _____ to the United States. (a) requisitioned (b) exported (c) bootlegged (d) imported **LO 1-1**   11._____

12. The United States' largest trading partner is _____. (a) Canada (b) Japan (c) China (d) Mexico **LO 1-1**   12._____

13. Which of the following is *not* a major U.S. export? (a) automobiles (b) bananas (c) computers (d) chemicals **LO 1-1**   13._____

14. Africa accounts for about _____ percent of all U.S. trade. (a) 25 (b) 12 (c) 6 (d) 3 **LO 1-1**   14._____

15. A country decides what to produce by considering _____. (a) the type of resources it has (b) the quality of resources it has (c) the amount of resources it has (d) all of these **LO 1-2**   15._____

16. The ability of a country to produce more of a good using the same or fewer resources as another country is called _____. (a) absolute advantage (b) opportunity cost (c) comparative advantage (d) allocation efficiency **LO 1-2**   16._____

17. A country can maximize the benefits of trade by _____. (a) importing all of its goods (b) exporting all of its goods (c) specializing in goods it produces with the lowest opportunity cost (d) none of these **LO 1-2**   17._____

18. In Utopia, it takes 50 labor hours to produce DVDs and 100 labor hours to produce oil. In   18._____
    Erewhon, it takes 200 labor hours to produce DVDs and 200 hours to produce oil. Which of
    the following statements is correct? (a) Erewhon has an absolute advantage in the production
    of oil. (b) Utopia should produce oil. (c) Utopia has a comparative advantage in the
    production of DVDs. (d) Erewhon has an absolute advantage in the production of both DVDs
    and oil. **LO 1-2**

19. Trade between the United States and Nicaragua _____. (a) benefits both countries   19._____
    (b) can never work to Nicaragua's advantage because U.S. workers are more productive
    (c) is a better deal for Nicaragua because labor is much cheaper there (d) should never occur
    under the theory of comparative advantage **LO 1-2**

20. If Utopia can produce two tons of coffee per day and Erewhon can produce one ton of coffee   20._____
    per day, then _____. (a) Utopia has a comparative advantage (b) Erewhon has an absolute
    advantage (c) Utopia has an absolute advantage (d) Erewhon has a comparative advantage
    LO 1-2

Part 3 Short Answer

Directions: Read the following questions, and write your response.

21. Identify at least four leading U.S. exports. Also name at least four leading U.S. imports. **LO 1-1**

22. Explain the relationship between opportunity cost, specialization, and trade. **LO 1-2**

Part 4 Critical Thinking

23. Use the information in the table below to answer the questions. **LO 1-2**

	Computers per hour	**Shirts per hour**
Utopia	300	200
Erewhon	400	300

Utopia has an absolute advantage in _____.

Erewhon has an absolute advantage in_____.

Utopia's opportunity cost of producing 100 extra shirts is _____.
Utopia's opportunity cost of producing 100 extra computers is _____.

Erewhon's opportunity cost of producing 100 extra shirts is _____.
Erewhon's opportunity cost of producing 100 extra computers is_____.

The comparative advantage for computers belongs to_____ and the comparative
advantage for shirts belongs to _____.

Based on their comparative advantages, Erewhon should specialize in producing _____and
Utopia should specialize in producing _____.

15-2 Barriers to Free Trade

Part 1 True or False

Directions: Place a *T* for True or an *F* for False in the Answers column to show whether each of the following statements is true or false.

Answers

1. In theory, global trade should be based on the principles of protectionism. **LO 2-1**   1. _____

2. Tariffs are the strongest type of trade barrier. **LO 2-1**   2. _____

3. Tariff rates are different for all products. **LO 2-1**   3. _____

4. A limit on the quantity of a good that can be imported in a given time period is called an *import allocation*. **LO 2-1**   4. _____

5. Quotas often cause other countries to adopt their own trade restrictions. **LO 2-1**   5. _____

6. Removing import barriers might save each American family a few hundred dollars every year. **LO 2-2**   6. _____

7. Economists generally agree that an "infant" industry is one that has existed between one and five years. **LO 2-2**   7. _____

8. The *national defense argument* for protectionism is much more relevant for the United States now than it was 50 or 60 years ago. **LO 2-2**   8. _____

9. The *protecting jobs argument* often saves jobs in one domestic industry at the expense of jobs in other domestic industries. **LO 2-2**   9. _____

10. A major flaw in the *cheap foreign labor argument* is that it neglects the reason for the differences in the wage rates between countries. **LO 2-2**   10. _____

Part 2 Multiple Choice

Directions: In the Answers column, write the letter that represents the word, or group of words, that correctly completes the statement or answers the question.

Answers

11. The flow of goods between countries without restrictions or special taxes is called _____.
    (a) global trade (b) barter (c) free trade (d) globalization **LO 2-1**   11. _____

12. This is a law that bars trade with another country. (a) boycott (b) injunction (c) sanction (d) embargo **LO 2-1**   12. _____

13. A tax on an import is called a(n) _____. (a) tariff (b) excise tax (c) levy (d) value-added tax **LO 2-1**   13. _____

14. This group was created in 1995 to enforce rulings on global trade disputes. (a) World Bank (b) World Trade Organization (c) European Union (d) General Agreement on Tariffs and Trade **LO 2-1**   14. _____

15. The current U.S. tariff code specifies tariffs on nearly _____ percent of U.S. imports. (a) 20 (b) 50 (c) 70 (d) 90 **LO 2-1**   15. _____

16. Trade restrictions can _____. (a) help some domestic workers keep their jobs (b) decrease competition (c) increase the price of goods for the consumer (d) all of these **LO 2-2**   16. _____

17. Proponents of the _____ suggest that a new domestic industry needs trade protection because it is not yet ready to compete with older, more established foreign competitors. (a) infant industry argument (b) immature trade theory (c) principle of comparative advantage (d) national security argument **LO 2-2**

17._____

18. The *national defense argument* for protectionism first came into prominence during _____. (a) the Revolutionary War (b) the War of 1812 (c) the Civil War (d) World War I **LO 2-2**

18._____

19. According to the *protecting jobs argument*, _____. (a) restricting exports increases domestic jobs (b) protectionism increases competition between domestic goods and imported goods (c) the sale of an imported good comes at the expense of a domestically produced good (d) all of these **LO 2-2**

19._____

20. When Vince complains that workers in Thailand make only $2 an hour while American workers in the same industry make $25 an hour, he is advancing which protectionist argument? (a) the cheap foreign labor argument (b) the fair-share argument (c) the one-percenter argument (d) the national defense argument **LO 2-2**

20._____

Part 3 Short Answer

Directions: Read the following questions, and write your response.

21. Define *protectionism*. **LO 2-1**

22. What is the primary reason why trade barriers exist? **LO 2-2**

23. What is the reason for the difference in wage rates between countries? **LO 2-2**

Part 4 Critical Thinking

Directions: Read the following questions, and write your response.

24. What effect does a tariff on imports to the United States have? **LO 2-1**

25. Who do trade restrictions help? Who do they harm? **LO 2-1**

26. Of the four main protectionist arguments discussed in your textbook, which do you think is the strongest? Explain your answer. **LO 2-2**

15-3 Measures of Trade

Part 1 True or False

Directions: Place a *T* for True or an *F* for False in the Answers column to show whether each of the following statements is true or false.

Answers

1. Exchange rates are less important than they used to be because the U.S. dollar has become the "universal currency of international business." **LO 3-1** 1._____

2. A fixed exchange rate is a system in which exchange rates are determined by the forces of supply and demand. **LO 3-1** 2._____

3. When the exchange rate is flexible, governments take a minimal role in foreign exchange markets. **LO 3-1** 3._____

4. If there is an increase in the dollar price of a Japanese yen, currency appreciation also occurs for the U.S. dollar. **LO 3-1** 4._____

5. A "weak" dollar is very bad news for U.S. producers. **LO 3-1** 5._____

6. Since 1975, the United States has experienced trade deficits. **LO 3-2** 6._____

7. If a country exports five boatloads of goods and imports only two boatloads of goods, then a trade surplus definitely exists. **LO 3-2** 7._____

8. Another term for *trade surplus* is *favorable balance of trade*. **LO 3-2** 8._____

9. Between 2005 and 2008, the rising price of imported oil greatly impacted the U.S. balance of trade. **LO 3-2** 9._____

10. As of 2011, the United States had free trade agreements with just two countries: Mexico and Canada. **LO 3-2** 10._____

Part 2 Multiple Choice

Directions: In the Answers column, write the letter that represents the word, or group of words, that correctly completes the statement or answers the question.

Answers

11. Suppose the exchange rate is 1.75 U.S. dollars = 1 British pound. If you are visiting London and purchase a scarf for 12 pounds, what would be the price of your purchase in dollars? (a) $6.86 (b) $13.75 (c) $21.00 (d) $22.61 **LO 3-1** 11._____

12. A(n) _____ exchange rate system is one in which exchange rates are held constant by a country's government. (a) fixed (b) gold-standard (c) neutral (d) expansionary **LO 3-1** 12._____

13. Exchange rates between most major currencies are _____. (a) arbitrary (b) pegged (c) flexible (d) fixed **LO 3-1** 13._____

14. As the dollar depreciates, _____. (a) U.S. exports become less expensive (b) U.S. imports become more expensive (c) U.S. imports decrease and U.S. exports increase (d) all of these **LO 3-1** 14._____

15. Suppose Nancy is visiting Europe next month. Because she plans to do lots of shopping on her trip, Nancy hopes for _____. (a) a fixed exchange rate (b) a "strong" dollar (c) a "strong" euro (d) a pegged exchange rate **LO 3-1** 15._____

16. What determines the exchange rate for the U.S. dollar? (a) the United States government (b) the governments of foreign nations (c) the New York Stock Exchange (d) the interaction of demand and supply for currencies **LO 3-1**   16._____

17. What must happen to create a trade deficit for the United States? (a) The value of imported goods and services is greater than the value of exported goods and services. (b) The U.S. exports more than it imports. (c) Imports hit a historic low point. (d) all of these **LO 3-2**   17._____

18. Which of the following would be included in the U.S. balance of trade? (a) Saudi Arabia purchases grain from the U.S. (b) The U.S. imports automobiles from Germany. (c) The U.S. sells light bulbs to Turkey. (d) all of these **LO 3-2**   18._____

19. With which nation does the United States currently have the greatest trade deficit? (a) Japan (b) China (c) Canada (d) Mexico **LO 3-2**   19._____

20. Which of these countries is *not* a party to the North American Free Trade Agreement? (a) Mexico (b) Canada (c) El Salvador (d) all of these countries are part of NAFTA **LO 3-2**   20._____

Part 3 Short Answer

Directions: Read the following questions, and write your response.

21. Define the term *exchange rate*. **LO 3-1**

22. Distinguish between *depreciation of currency* and *appreciation of currency*. Explain the effect of each on U.S. exports and imports. **LO 3-1**

23. How is balance of trade calculated? **LO 3-2**

Part 4 Critical Thinking

Directions: Read the following questions, and write your response.

24. Why might a country choose to fix the value of its currency rather than use a flexible exchange system? **LO 3-1**

25. Do you believe a growing trade deficit is a problem for the U.S. economy? Why or why not? **LO 3-2**

Chapter 15 Review

Part 1 True or False

Directions: Place a *T* for True or an *F* for False in the Answers column to show whether each of the following statements is true or false.

Answers

1. The speed of transportation and communication forces today's producers to compete on a global basis. **LO 1-1**

   1._____

2. An *import* is a good produced in one country and purchased by another country. **LO 1-1**

   2._____

3. *Absolute advantage* is the ability of a country to produce more of a good using the same or fewer resources as another country. **LO 1-2**

   3._____

4. Every nation in the world protects its own domestic producers to some degree from foreign competition. **LO 2-1**

   4._____

5. Average U.S. tariff rates are higher now than at any time in history. **LO 2-1**

   5._____

6. The *infant industry argument* for protectionism has strong support among most economists. **LO 2-2**

   6._____

7. The *cheap labor argument* for protectionism ignores the fact that U.S. workers are generally more productive than workers in less developed nations. **LO 2-2**

   7._____

8. For most of the years between World War II and 1971, currency exchange rates were fixed. **LO 3-1**

   8._____

9. Before 1971, exchange rates were based primarily on silver. **LO 3-1**

   9._____

10. The stronger dollar has put the price of U.S. goods out of reach for many Mexican consumers. **LO 3-2**

   10._____

Part 2 Multiple Choice

Directions: In the Answers column, write the letter that represents the word, or group of words, that correctly completes the statement or answers the question.

Answers

11. Which of these countries is *not* a large trading partner with the United States? (a) Japan (b) Mexico (c) China (d) all of these countries are large U.S. trading partners **LO 1-1**

   11._____

12. Comparative advantage is found by _____. (a) comparing the relative opportunity costs (b) calculating the total cost of production (c) comparing labor costs of one to that of the other (d) none of these **LO 1-2**

   12._____

13. If countries specialize in producing certain goods, the result is _____. (a) worldwide inflation (b) total world production increases (c) increased unemployment (d) worldwide shortages of goods **LO 1-2**

   13._____

14. What is the most popular and visible measure used to discourage trade? (a) embargo (b) tariff (c) luxury tax (d) boycott **LO 2-1**

   14._____

15. The purpose of GATT is to _____. (a) protect domestic producers (b) provide low-cost starter loans to infant industries in developing countries (c) reduce tariff rates among member nations (d) enforce rulings on global trade disputes **LO 2-1**

   15._____

16. Suppose the Boeing Company—a major U.S. aerospace and defense corporation founded in 1916—is lobbying Washington for protection from foreign competition. Which argument would Boeing be *least* likely to make? (a) the infant industry argument (b) the national security argument (c) the protecting jobs argument (d) the cheap labor argument **LO 2-2**   16._____

17. Protectionism _____. (a) does sometimes save jobs in select domestic industries (b) often results in consumers paying higher prices (c) reduces foreign competition (d) all of these **LO 2-2**   17._____

18. Why did the value of the dollar begin to "float"? (a) The dollar became the "universal currency for international business" (b) Supply and demand no longer dictated the dollar's value. (c) The value of the dollar was no longer tied to gold. (d) none of these **LO 3-1**   18._____

19. A German camera company exports much of its output to the United States. This company is happiest when _____. (a) exchange rates are fixed (b) the dollar is "strong" (c) the dollar is "weak" (d) the euro is "strong" **LO 3-1**   19._____

20. The United States last experienced a trade surplus in _____. (a) 1955 (b) 1975 (c) 2005 (d) 2010 **LO 3-2**   20._____

Part 3 Short Answer

Directions: Read the following questions, and write your response.

21. The owner of a bicycle shop must pay a tariff of 25% on each French-made bicycle he buys to sell in his shop. The most popular imported bike sold in his store has a declared value of $300. What is the cost to the owner for the $300 bike? **LO 2-1**

22. If today's exchange rate is 1.85 U.S. dollars = 1 British pound, how many British pounds equals one U.S. dollar? **LO 3-1**

Part 4 Critical Thinking

Directions: Read the following question, and write your response.

23. Suppose the United States passed a law prohibiting the sale of all foreign goods. Explain how this would impact your life. **LO 1-1**

Chapter 15 International Trade

16-1 Rent or Own a Home

Part 1 True or False

Directions: Place a *T* for True or an *F* for False in the Answers column to show whether each of the following statements is true or false.

Answers

1. Some residential colleges and universities do not allow younger students to live off campus. **LO 1-1**

   1. _____

2. A *duplex* is one large room that serves as kitchen, living room, and bedroom. **LO 1-1**

   2. _____

3. The major advantage of living in a condominium is that your meals are provided for you. **LO 1-1**

   3. _____

4. As a renter, your monthly rent is not tax-deductible. **LO 1-1**

   4. _____

5. A single family residence is the typical choice for people buying homes. **LO 1-2**

   5. _____

6. The value of most homes depreciates over time. **LO 1-2**

   6. _____

7. Keeping your home in good condition can increase the value of your neighbors' property as well as the value of your own home. **LO 1-2**

   7. _____

8. The buyer usually pays the real estate agent's sales commission fee. **LO 1-3**

   8. _____

9. If a home inspection reveals significant damage, the seller generally pays the cost of repairs before the sale is made final. **LO 1-3**

   9. _____

10. A mortgage payment includes both principal and interest. **LO 1-3**

    10. _____

Part 2 Multiple Choice

Directions: In the Answers column, write the letter that represents the word, or group of words, that correctly completes the statement or answers the question.

Answers

11. All of the following are on-campus housing options *except* _____. (a) sorority house (b) dormitory (c) townhouse (d) fraternity house **LO 1-1**

    11. _____

12. Which of these would most likely be the least expensive housing option? (a) studio apartment (b) townhouse (c) condominium (d) duplex **LO 1-1**

    12. _____

13. Which statement about renting is *correct*? (a) Tenants are usually responsible for the cost of maintenance and repairs. (b) Few rental properties offer laundry, mail, or other services. (c) Tenants must give written notice before they move out of rental property. (d) Most rental properties are furnished. **LO 1-1**

    13. _____

14. A refundable sum of money that assures a tenant meets the terms of the rental agreement is called _____. (a) collateral (b) a deposit (c) rent (d) a mortgage payment **LO 1-1**

    14. _____

15. The difference between what you owe for your home and the amount for which you could sell the property is called _____. (a) owner's assets (b) principal (c) capital gains (d) equity **LO 1-2**

    15. _____

16. When you own a home, _____. (a) you must obey all local zoning laws (b) your utility bills will likely be less than when you rented (c) you will no longer need to pay property taxes (d) all of these **LO 1-2**

    16. _____

17. The process of taking away private property to pay for debts levied against it is called _____. (a) garnishment (b) eminent domain (c) foreclosure (d) recapture **LO 1-2**   17._____

18. If you buy a home that costs $100,000, you can expect to pay a down payment of between _____. (a) $2,000 to $5,000 (b) $5,000 to $10,000 (c) $10,000 to $20,000 (d) $20,000 to $40,000 **LO 1-3**   18._____

19. Expenses incurred in transferring ownership to the person purchasing a home are called _____. (a) closing costs (b) installation fees (c) moving costs (d) escrow payments **LO 1-3**   19._____

20. Combining telephone, cable TV, and Internet service into a single, money-saving package from one company is called _____. (a) upselling (b) prorating (c) wrapping (d) bundling **LO 1-3**   20._____

Part 3 Short Answer

Directions: Read the following questions, and write your response.

21. What are some advantages to on-campus housing? **LO 1-1**

22. Identify and briefly describe several specific fees and deposits that renters must often pay. **LO 1-1**

23. How can a homeowner avoid paying capital gains tax when he or she sells the home? **LO 1-2**

Part 4 Critical Thinking

Directions: Read the following question, and write your response.

24. Moving into a new home can be expensive. What are some ways you can think of to reduce the cost of moving into a new home? **LO 1-3**

16-2 Lease or Buy a Car

Part 1 True or False

Directions: Place a *T* for True or an *F* for False in the Answers column to show whether each of the following statements is true or false.

Answers

1. If you agree with the phrase "Buy assets that appreciate, rent assets that depreciate," then you would never consider leasing a car. **LO 2-1**

1. _____

2. People who lease a car usually start a new lease for a new vehicle every two to three years. **LO 2-1**

2. _____

3. When your car lease expires, you will be obligated to purchase the vehicle—but for a reduced price. **LO 2-1**

3. _____

4. If you purchase a hybrid vehicle, you may be eligible for a tax credit. **LO 2-1**

4. _____

5. *Automobile insurance* is a guarantee that if something goes wrong with your new car, the manufacturer covers the cost of repairs. **LO 2-1**

5. _____

6. Do not be in a hurry when shopping for a car. **LO 2-2**

6. _____

7. Be prepared to walk away from a potential vehicle purchase if you cannot negotiate a reasonable price with the seller. **LO 2-2**

7. _____

8. A 24-month auto loan will cost you more interest than a 48-month auto loan, but your monthly payments will be lower. **LO 2-2**

8. _____

9. Not making your car payments on time can lead to *foreclosure* of your vehicle. **LO 2-2**

9. _____

10. When you buy a new car, the car will likely decrease in value faster than your loan amount. **LO 2-2**

10. _____

Part 2 Multiple Choice

Directions: In the Answers column, write the letter that represents the word, or group of words, that correctly completes the statement or answers the question.

Answers

11. Parker has decided to lease a new Ford Focus from Northside Auto Sales. Janice, a Northside salesperson, helps Parker fill out all the necessary paperwork, and then presents him with the keys to the vehicle. In this scenario, who is the *lessee*? (a) Janice (b) Parker (c) Northside Auto Sales (d) the Ford Motor Company **LO 2-1**

11. _____

12. If you decide to lease a car, you _____. (a) will need to make only a relatively small down payment (b) can drive the car as many miles as you want without paying any penalty (c) are responsible for paying for all repairs, both major and minor (d) all of these **LO 2-1**

12. _____

13. If you are a business owner, it makes sense for you to lease a vehicle if you _____. (a) need a new car every couple of years (b) intend to buy the vehicle once the lease expires (c) rarely need to drive for business purposes (d) are not interested in using the leasing costs as a tax shelter **LO 2-1**

13. _____

14. Most car loans today are for _____ years. (a) one to two (b) two to three (c) three to five (d) five to seven **LO 2-1**

14. _____

15. A typical factory warranty for a car covers buyers for the first _____ miles or _____ years. (a) 10,000; two (b) 25,000; three (c) 36,000; three (d) 50,000; five **LO 2-1**

15. _____

16. The vehicle identification number can be especially important to have when you _____.   16. _____
(a) are buying a used car (b) want to get preapproved for a vehicle loan (c) are comparing insurance rates (d) all of these **LO 2-2**

17. You can check out the average price of a used car in the _____. (a) NADA Guides   17. _____
(b) latest issue of *Car & Driver* magazine (c) *Kelley Blue Book* (d) database of vehicles maintained by your state's Department of Motor Vehicles **LO 2-2**

18. You might consider using a car buying service if you _____. (a) have not been pre-   18. _____
qualified for a vehicle loan (b) have poor negotiation skills (c) are leasing rather than buying a vehicle (d) are unsure of the insurance premiums for the vehicle you have chosen **LO 2-2**

19. Which of these is *not* a good idea to follow when you are shopping for a new car? (a) test   19. _____
drive the car (b) research potential vehicles both online and in person (c) include as many dealer add-ons as you can afford (d) set a spending limit and stick to it **LO 2-2**

20. The best way to buy a car is _____. (a) with cash (b) through your bank or credit union   20. _____
(c) with a credit card (d) directly through the car dealership **LO 2-2**

Part 3 Short Answer

Directions: Read the following questions, and write your response.

21. What is a *car lease*? **LO 2-1**

22. What is a *sales finance company*? **LO 2-2**

Part 4 Critical Thinking

Directions: Read the following question, and write your response.

23. Why is it a good idea to be preapproved for a vehicle loan when you are shopping for a new car? **LO 2-2**

24. If you purchased a new vehicle, would you buy an extended warranty plan? Why or why not? **LO 2-2**

Chapter 16 Build Assets and Wealth

16-3 Risk Management and Insurance

Part 1 True or False

Directions: Place a *T* for True or an *F* for False in the Answers column to show whether each of the following statements is true or false.

Answers

1. All risks are avoidable. **LO 3-1** 1._____

2. The process of assessing risks and planning actions to reduce and avoid the losses that could occur is called *risk management*. **LO 3-1** 2._____

3. With *risk reduction*, you stop the behavior to avoid the risk. **LO 3-1** 3._____

4. Joaquin understands that there is a slight risk that he might be hit in the head by a foul ball if he goes to the baseball game tonight. Nevertheless, he decides to attend the game anyway. In this case, Joaquin is *assuming* the risk. **LO 3-1** 4._____

5. With self-insuring, you set aside money to be used in the event of injury or loss; if loss occurs, you take money from the cash set aside to pay for the loss. **LO 3-2** 5._____

6. Unlike homeowners, renters do not need property insurance because the landlord is liable for any damage to tenants' personal belongings. **LO 3-2** 6._____

7. If you take out a loan to buy a car, the creditor will require you to carry full insurance coverage on your vehicle. **LO 3-2** 7._____

8. A *co-pay* is the amount of money you have to pay before insurance begins to pay for services. **LO 3-2** 8._____

9. *Disability insurance* typically replaces 100 percent of normal income earnings when the insured is unable to work due to a work-related injury or illness. **LO 3-2** 9._____

10. With a flexible spending account, money is set aside pre-tax and can be used to pay medical costs not paid by insurance. One downside, however, is that money withheld but not spent by year-end is forfeited. **LO 3-2** 10._____

Part 2 Multiple Choice

Directions: In the Answers column, write the letter that represents the word, or group of words, that correctly completes the statement or answers the question.

Answers

11. The chance of injury, damage, or economic loss is called _____. (a) peril (b) risk (c) probability (d) threat **LO 3-1** 11._____

12. Which of the following would best be categorized as a *personal risk*? (a) losing precious family photos (b) incurring exorbitant medical bills (c) your investments losing their value (d) lending a friend money and not being repaid **LO 3-1** 12._____

13. The first step in risk management is to _____. (a) assess the probability of the risk (b) take action to minimize the risk (c) identify your risks and what you could lose (d) prioritize the risks based on the possible consequences **LO 3-1** 13._____

14. Which risk strategy are you following when you purchase insurance? (a) transfer risk (b) assume risk (c) avoid risk (d) none of these **LO 3-1** 14._____

15. It is sometimes acceptable to use the risk _____ strategy if the risk of personal and financial loss is low and not serious. (a) reduction (b) assumption (c) avoidance (d) transfer **LO 3-1**   15._____

16. This type of auto insurance protects others from injuries caused by an accident that is your fault. (a) liability coverage (b) collision coverage (c) comprehensive coverage (d) no-fault insurance **LO 3-2**   16._____

17. A _____ is a network of independent health care providers that work together to provide health services. (a) preferred provider organization (b) fee-for-service association (c) health maintenance organization (d) major medical group **LO 3-2**   17._____

18. _____ is a temporary insurance policy that provides death benefits for a period of time, such as 20 years. (a) Whole life insurance (b) Term life insurance (c) Universal life insurance (d) Endowment life insurance **LO 3-2**   18._____

19. Which of the following will likely help you reduce the cost of insurance? (a) lowering your deductible (b) paying premiums monthly rather than annually (c) having more than one policy with the same insurance company (d) all of these **LO 3-2**   19._____

20. Once you have insurance, how often should you compare premiums and coverage? (a) every six months (b) annually (c) at least every three years (d) when you reach major life milestones **LO 3-2**   20._____

Part 3 Short Answer

Directions: Read the following questions, and write your response.

21. Identify the four risk strategies that help you manage risks. **LO 3-1**

22. What is *stacking* and how does it affect the cost of insurance? **LO 3-2**

23. What is included in *full coverage* motor vehicle insurance? **LO 3-2**

Part 4 Critical Thinking

Directions: Read the following question, and write your response.

24. Give an example from your personal experience in which you reduced, avoided, or assumed a risk. Why did you handle the risk in this manner? **LO 3-1**

25. Montez is a 20-year old single man with no children or dependents. Does it make sense for him to purchase life insurance? Why or why not? **LO 3-2**

16-4 Purchase, Use, and Dispose of Property

Part 1 True or False

Directions: Place a *T* for True or an *F* for False in the Answers column to show whether each of the following statements is true or false.

Answers

1. When you buy property, you are purchasing an asset—an item of value that will change in value over time. **LO 4-1**

   1._____

2. A positive cash flow means your costs are greater than your revenues. **LO 4-1**

   2._____

3. Buying or leasing personal property is more complicated than buying or leasing commercial property or real property. **LO 4-1**

   3._____

4. The ownership of private property is one of the hallmarks of a free enterprise economy. **LO 4-1**

   4._____

5. By law, only a licensed real estate agent can sell real property. **LO 4-1**

   5._____

6. When property is sold, a transfer tax is sometimes assessed against the seller of the property. **LO 4-1**

   6._____

7. When you own property, you can use it any way you wish. **LO 4-2**

   7._____

8. If property taxes are unpaid, the money owed accumulates as a lien. **LO 4-2**

   8._____

9. If land is zoned residential, it cannot be developed for business activity. **LO 4-2**

   9._____

10. A title report includes any debt or other liens attached to a piece of property. **LO 4-2**

    10._____

Part 2 Multiple Choice

Directions: In the Answers column, write the letter that represents the word, or group of words, that correctly completes the statement or answers the question.

Answers

11. A comparison of features, size, location and other similar properties to determine a fair price of an asset is called a(n) _____. (a) appraisal (b) evaluation (c) auction (d) valuation **LO 4-1**

    11._____

12. All of the following would be considered personal property *except* your _____. (a) pick-up truck (b) house (c) sofa (d) wedding ring **LO 4-1**

    12._____

13. Assets a business uses to generate income are called _____ property. (a) market (b) real (c) corporate (d) commercial **LO 4-1**

    13._____

14. If you own a house, you must pay _____ taxes. (a) excise (b) real estate (c) property (d) homeowner's **LO 4-1**

    14._____

15. Three years ago, the Sexton Corporation purchased a computer system for $2,000. The computer system has depreciated in value by $1,600. What is the current *book value* of the computer system? (a) $2,000 (b) $1,600 (c) $1,000 (d) $400 **LO 4-1**

    15._____

16. A listing agreement is a _____. (a) legal obligation that must be paid before a clear title to property can be passed to a new owner (b) record of ownership and all legal restrictions on a property (c) legal contract that describes the property being sold, the price being asked, and the sales commission (d) legal right of another entity to have limited use of property **LO 4-1**

    16._____

17. A title report is a _____. (a) legal obligation that must be paid before a clear title to property   17._____
can be passed to a new owner (b) record of ownership and all legal restrictions on a property
(c) legal contract that describes the property being sold, the price being asked, and the sales
commission (d) legal right of another entity to have limited use of property **LO 4-2**

18. Marsha has a(n) _____ with a neighbor, Abraham, that allows her to use a path through   18._____
Abraham's woods to reach her house on the other side of the woods. (a) easement (b) lien
(c) CCR (d) property accord **LO 4-2**

19. These types of laws restrict the type of construction as well as the purpose of a lot or other   19._____
real property. (a) building codes (b) zoning laws (c) CCRs (d) commercial property laws
LO 4-2

20. This is the legal surrender of private property for public use. (a) habeas corpus   20._____
(b) appropriation (c) eminent domain (d) compulsory purchase **LO 4-2**

Part 3 Short Answer

Directions: Read the following questions, and write your response.

21. Define the term *wealth*. **LO 4-1**

22. What is a homeowners' association? What is the function of such an organization? **LO 4-2**

Part 4 Critical Thinking

Directions: Read the following questions, and write your response.

23. Do you believe the government should be allowed to exercise the power of eminent domain? Explain
your answer. **LO 4-2**

Chapter 16 Build Assets and Wealth

Chapter 16 Review

Part 1 True or False

Directions: Place a *T* for True or an *F* for False in the Answers column to show whether each of the following statements is true or false.

Answers

1. A *townhouse* is one large room that serves as kitchen, living room, and bedroom **LO 1-1** 1._____

2. Tenants can be forced to move out if they do not obey the terms of the rental agreement. **LO 1-1** 2._____

3. Because property taxes and interest on home loans are tax deductible, home ownership is considered a tax shelter. **LO 1-2** 3._____

4. An FHA loan is guaranteed by mortgage insurance premiums paid on the loan. **LO 1-3** 4._____

5. A major disadvantage of leasing a car is that you never have to pay off the vehicle. **LO 2-1** 5._____

6. Dealer add-ons are high-priced, high-profit dealer services that add little or no value. **LO 2-2** 6._____

7. The likelihood of a risk actually turning into a loss is called *probability*. **LO 3-1** 7._____

8. Whole life insurance is considered "pure insurance" because you aren't paying for anything other than insurance. **LO 3-2** 8._____

9. A *cash flow* is the net amount you receive over and above the costs you have to pay. **LO 4-1** 9._____

10. A housing subdivision may require that a homeowner must use a certain type of building material if he or she builds a deck in the backyard. **LO 4-2** 10._____

Part 2 Multiple Choice

Directions: In the Answers column, write the letter that represents the word, or group of words, that correctly completes the statement or answers the question.

Answers

11. A _____ is an on-campus building that contains furnished rooms rented to students. (a) dormitory (b) studio apartment (c) duplex (d) condominium **LO 1-1** 11._____

12. Which of the following is tax deductible for homeowners? (a) equity (b) principal on home loans (c) property taxes (d) maintenance expenses **LO 1-2** 12._____

13. Mortgages can be for any number of years, but are usually for _____ years or _____ years. (a) 5; 10 (b) 10; 20 (c) 15; 30 (d) 20; 40 **LO 1-3** 13._____

14. If you lease a car, for which of the following would you be required to pay? (a) rebuild the engine (b) change the oil (c) replace the transmission (d) all of these **LO 2-1** 14._____

15. General Motors Acceptance Corporation is an example of a _____. (a) bank (b) auto dealership (c) credit union (d) sales finance company **LO 2-2** 15._____

16. Danielle has always wanted to own a home on the beach in Mathews County, Virginia. But when she learned that Mathews County has a devastating hurricane visit at least once every five years, she decided to find another beachfront location for her dream home. In this case, Danielle is _____ the risk. (a) transferring (b) avoiding (c) assuming (d) reducing **LO 3-1** 16._____

17. If a hailstorm damages your vehicle, this type of insurance will help pay for repairs.   17. _____
    (a) liability coverage (b) collision coverage (c) personal injury protection (d) comprehensive
    coverage **LO 3-2**

18. Marco has a health insurance plan with a $500 deductible. He pays 20% of all costs after the   18. _____
    deductible is met. If he has a medical bill of $2,000, how much will Marco pay out-of-pocket?
    (a) $900 (b) $800 (c) $500 (d) $400 **LO 3-2**

19. The appraisal for income property includes _____. (a) analysis of the income potential and   19. _____
    costs (b) vacancy rates (c) projected market conditions (d) all of these **LO 4-1**

20. A lien is a _____. (a) legal obligation that must be paid before a clear title to property can be   20. _____
    passed to a new owner (b) record of ownership and all legal restrictions on a property (c) legal
    contract that describes the property being sold, the price being asked, and the sales commission
    (d) legal right of another entity to have limited use of property **LO 4-2**

Part 3 Short Answer

Directions: Read the following questions, and write your response.

21. What is a *mortgage*? What is an *escrow account*? **LO 1-3**

22. Distinguish between *basic health care insurance* and *major medical coverage*. **LO 3-2**

Part 4 Critical Thinking

Directions: Read the following questions, and write your response.

23. If you were looking for a new car, would you lease or would you buy? Explain your answer. **LO 2-1**

24. A homeowners' association may have the power to determine the color of your home, the number of pets
    you have, or the type of grass you have to plant. Do you think this is fair? Why or why not? **LO 4-2**

17-1 Invest in Stocks

Part 1 True or False

Directions: Place a *T* for True or an *F* for False in the Answers column to show whether each of the following statements is true or false.

Answers

1. The first purpose of saving should be to accumulate wealth. **LO 1-1**   1._____

2. The purchase of stocks from individual companies is a form of *indirect investing.* **LO 1-1**   2._____

3. A group of different types of investments is called a portfolio. **LO 1-1**   3._____

4. The process of selecting different types of investments with different levels of risk is called *investment equilibrium.* **LO 1-1**   4._____

5. A corporation receives funds only when stock is first sold; when you buy stock from a current owner, the corporation does not receive more funds. **LO 1-1**   5._____

6. An *investment club* is a professionally managed group of investments. **LO 1-2**   6._____

7. An individual retirement account uses money its members provide to invest in stocks or bonds. **LO 1-2**   7._____

8. All forms of investing come with some risk. **LO 1-2**   8._____

9. When you invest indirectly, you rely on the expertise of professionals who manage investments for a living. **LO 1-2**   9._____

10. A *capital gain* is one of the worst things that can happen to an investor. **LO 1-2**   10._____

Part 2 Multiple Choice

Directions: In the Answers column, write the letter that represents the word, or group of words, that correctly completes the statement or answers the question.

Answers

11. An amount of money available for unplanned expenses is called a(n) _____.
    (a) emergency fund (b) mutual fund (c) trust fund (d) slush fund **LO 1-1**   11._____

12. The sale of corporate stock to generate cash is _____. (a) equity financing (b) debt assumption (c) asset allocation (d) debt financing **LO 1-1**   12._____

13. Which type of investment risk is probably the most unpredictable? (a) industry risk (b) political risk (c) inflation risk (d) stock risk **LO 1-1**   13._____

14. Which of the following is an example of stock risk? (a) You buy stock at $30 per share and at the end of the year the stock is worth $33 per share; however, the annual inflation rate is 12 percent. (b) You invest in a company in the oil business, but your investment begins to lose value as alternate sources of energy are developed. (c) Your investment in an oceanfront office complex seemed like a good idea, until a hurricane destroyed the facility. (d) Not long after investing in the Palmer Corporation, the company is rocked by a financial scandal that sends the company into bankruptcy. **LO 1-1**   14._____

15. Which diversification strategy involves buying stocks at a low price and selling when the price is high? (a) dollar-cost averaging (b) investment tracking (c) market timing (d) comparison shopping **LO 1-1**   15._____

16. Which of the following is a form of *indirect investing*? (a) purchasing mutual funds (b) joining an investment club (c) opening an IRA (d) none of these **LO 1-2**   16._____

17. This type of mutual fund is considered medium risk. (a) global fund (b) income fund (c) balanced fund (d) bond fund **LO 1-2**   17._____

18. Martha wants an investment that produces a steady and reliable dividend. Which type of mutual fund would be a good choice for her? (a) precious metal fund (b) income fund (c) new venture fund (d) growth fund **LO 1-2**   18._____

19. The process of choosing a combination of funds that can be found in different mutual funds is called _____. (a) asset allocation (b) diversification (c) investment tracking (d) debt financing **LO 1-2**   19._____

20. A(n) _____ is a type of investment purchased through a life insurance company that pays a fixed return; the underlying investment supports the payments you will receive in the future. (a) allowance (b)bond (c) annuity (d) pension **LO 1-2**   20._____

Part 3 Short Answer

Directions: Read the following questions, and write your response.

21. What is investment risk? How can you offset investment risk? **LO 1-1/LO 1-2**

22. Identify one low-risk mutual fund, one medium-risk fund, and one high-risk fund. **LO 1-2**

Part 4 Critical Thinking

Directions: Read the following questions, and write your response.

23. How does investing in stocks support economic growth? **LO 1-2**

24. Suppose a wealthy relative has left you an inheritance of $5,000. You decide to invest this money in mutual funds. What type of mutual fund would you choose? Would you allocate your assets? If so, how? Explain your answer. **LO 1-2**

17-2 Invest in Bonds

Part 1 True or False

Directions: Place a *T* for True or an *F* for False in the Answers column to show whether each of the following statements is true or false.

Answers

1. Notes payable is considered a form of long-term debt. **LO 2-1**   1._____

2. When a bond *matures*, the full amount of principal and interest must be paid. **LO 2-1**   2._____

3. Bond rating services such as Moody's and Standard and Poor's rate bonds based on their face value. **LO 2-1**   3._____

4. A *participating bond* is attractive to investors because the potential return is greater while the risk does not rise. **LO 2-1**   4._____

5. Suppose in 2012 you purchased a ten-year, $1,000 bond at a fixed rate of 5 percent. In 2013, interest rates drop. In this case, the value of your bond has decreased. **LO 2-1**   5._____

6. The federal government as well as local and state governments issue government bonds. **LO 2-2**   6._____

7. A *general-obligation bond* is a municipal bond issued to raise money for a public-works project such as airports or hospitals. **LO 2-2**   7._____

8. An *I bond* is a type of savings bond that is sold at one-half its face value. **LO 2-2**   8._____

9. A treasury bill is a long-term security with a maturity date of 30 years. **LO 2-2**   9._____

10. For purposes of risk management, investing in U.S. government securities is the safest form of investing possible. **LO 2-2**   10._____

Part 2 Multiple Choice

Directions: In the Answers column, write the letter that represents the word, or group of words, that correctly completes the statement or answers the question.

Answers

11. What is the face value of a $1,000, ten-year, 5 percent bond? (a) $50 (b) $500 (c) $1,000 (d) $10,000 **LO 2-1**   11._____

12. This type of corporate bond is based on the general creditworthiness of the company. (a) secured bond (b) serial bond (c) convertible bond (d) debenture **LO 2-1**   12._____

13. A zero-coupon bond _____. (a) has no annual interest payments (b) decreases in value as the bond ages (c) is a form of debt from companies that don't have an investment grade rating (d) all of these **LO 2-1**   13._____

14. Suppose a corporation issues a ten-year, $10 million, 5 percent bond. The annual interest is $500,000. Each year, the corporation pays interest as well as 1/10 of the principal. What type of bond is this? (a) term bond (b) serial bond (c) annuity (d) junk bond **LO 2-1**   14._____

15. A callable bond _____. (a) usually sells at a higher price than other bonds (b) can be exchanged for shares of stock at a preset date or within a preset period of time (c) shares in profits of the corporation (d) can be paid off at a preset date or within a preset period of time **LO 2-1**   15._____

16. Which of the following statements about corporate bonds is *incorrect*? (a) The market price 16._____
of a bond is fixed. (b) All corporate bonds are issued with a stated face value. (c) The interest
rate on a bond is fixed. (d) Earnings on bonds are computed at simple interest rates. **LO 2-1**

17. A municipal bond _____. (a) usually has a minimum investment of $5,000 (b) is issued 17._____
by the federal government (c) generally pays a higher interest rate than a corporate bond
(d) all of these **LO 2-2**

18. A Series EE bond with a face value of $10,000 would be sold for _____. (a) $2,500 18._____
(b) $5,000 (c) $7,500 (d) $10,000 **LO 2-2**

19. A treasury note has a maturity date _____. (a) ranging from 4 to 52 weeks (b) of one year 19._____
(c) ranging from two to ten years (d) of 30 years **LO 2-2**

20. The Federal Housing Administration would issue which type of bond? (a) agency bond 20._____
(b) revenue bond (c) savings bond (d) treasury bond **LO 2-2**

Part 3 Short Answer

Directions: Read the following questions, and write your response.

21. Are bonds considered a safe or risky investment choice? Explain. **LO 2-1**

22. Identify the four types of government bonds. **LO 2-2**

Part 4 Critical Thinking

23. Complete the information in the table below for a $5,000 corporate bond with a fixed interest rate of 6
percent and a tax-exempt $5,000 municipal bond with a fixed interest rate of 5 percent. **LO 2-1**

	Corporate Bond	**Municipal Bond**
Face value	$5,000	$5,000
Fixed interest rate	6%	5%
Annual interest earnings		
Tax on earnings (25 %)		
Net interest earnings after tax		

17-3 Other Investing Options

Part 1 True or False

Directions: Place a *T* for True or an *F* for False in the Answers column to show whether each of the following statements is true or false.

Answers

1. Over the long run, real estate values have kept pace—if not exceeded—the annual inflation rate. **LO 3-1**

   1. _____

2. Most investors buying speculative properties are unable to get bank financing because of the risk involved. **LO 3-1**

   2. _____

3. Rental property cannot be depreciated. **LO 3-1**

   3. _____

4. It is generally the renter's responsibility to maintain a rental property in a habitable condition. **LO 3-1**

   4. _____

5. All real estate investment is considered direct investment. **LO 3-1**

   5. _____

6. Investments in metals and gems are usually considered speculative. **LO 3-2**

   6. _____

7. Both precious metals and gems have their greatest retail value as jewelry. **LO 3-2**

   7. _____

8. The gems market is risky and unpredictable, but it is also fairly large and therefore easy for sellers to find potential buyers. **LO 3-2**

   8. _____

9. Commodities include farm products such as wheat, corn, or cattle as well as precious metals such as gold or silver. **LO 3-2**

   9. _____

10. Only people with money to lose should purchase futures. **LO 3-2**

   10. _____

Part 2 Multiple Choice

Directions: In the Answers column, write the letter that represents the word, or group of words, that correctly completes the statement or answers the question.

Answers

11. If an investment is *illiquid*, it _____. (a) does not keep pace with the annual rate of inflation (b) is considered virtually risk-free (c) can be difficult to sell in the short run (d) all of these **LO 3-1**

    11. _____

12. Vacant land is often considered a *speculative* investment because _____. (a) the investor is hoping that at some time in the future it will increase in value (b) it is sometimes hard to sell quickly (c) it almost always results in high profits for the investor (d) investors generally have no trouble obtaining financing for such purchases **LO 3-1**

    12. _____

13. Which of the following *cannot* be purchased as a rental property? (a) a single-family house (b) an apartment building (c) a condominium (d) all of these can be rental properties **LO 3-1**

    13. _____

14. A real estate syndicate _____. (a) is a type of non-profit corporation (b) generally invests in just one type of property (c) is a form of limited partnership (d) is an investment in a pool of mortgages that were purchased by a government agency **LO 3-1**

    14. _____

15. Which of these is most like a mutual fund? (a) a participation certificate (b) a real estate investment trust (c) a real estate syndicate (d) the purchase of rental property **LO 3-1**

    15. _____

16. All of the following are examples of precious metals *except* _____. (a) gold (b) rubies (c) silver (d) platinum **LO 3-2**

    16. _____

17. Investments in precious metals _____. (a) vary greatly in price over time (b) are considered very liquid (c) are usually easy to sell quickly (d) can provide a steady, current income **LO 3-2**   17. _____

18. When you buy gems and precious metals at retail prices, you are paying markups as high as _____ percent or higher. (a) 500 (b) 100 (c) 50 (d) 25 **LO 3-2**   18. _____

19. What is the most commonly collected item? (a) gems (b) baseball cards (c) stamps (d) coins **LO 3-2**   19. _____

20. A contract to buy and sell commodities or stocks for a specified price on a specified date in the future is called a(n) _____. (a) annuity (b) put option (c) future (d) call option **LO 3-2**   20. _____

Part 3 Short Answer

Directions: Read the following questions, and write your response.

21. What is a *participation certificate*? **LO 3-1**

22. Explain why the commodity prices are volatile. **LO 3-2**

23. What are *collectibles*? What makes collectibles valuable? **LO 3-2**

Part 4 Critical Thinking

Directions: Read the following question, and write your response.

24. Glenda and Stan live in Ohio. They purchased a second home in Florida to use for family vacations and special events. When they are not using the property themselves, Glenda and Stan rent it out to generate additional income. Discuss some ways this could turn out to be a costly investment for this couple. **LO 3-1**

17-4 Retirement Planning and Philanthropy

Part 1 True or False

Directions: Place a *T* for True or an *F* for False in the Answers column to show whether each of the following statements is true or false.

Answers

1. The only way to open a retirement account is through your employer. **LO 4-1**

    1. ____

2. You are responsible for managing an IRA account. These types of accounts are not professionally managed. **LO 4-1**

    2. ____

3. All income earned in a Roth IRA is tax-free. **LO 4-1**

    3. ____

4. A Keogh account is a tax-deferred retirement plan for employees of large corporations. **LO 4-1**

    4. ____

5. Defined-benefit plans are offered by more companies now than in the past. **LO 4-1**

    5. ____

6. One major advantage to retirement is that all of your living expenses will fall significantly. **LO 4-2**

    6. ____

7. Life insurance proceeds are part of your estate—unless a specific beneficiary is named. **LO 4-2**

    7. ____

8. A *guardianship* is often set up for heirs who are minors. **LO 4-2**

    8. ____

9. *Giving circles* are groups of individuals who become friends and pool their charitable donations. **LO 4-2**

    9. ____

10. A foundation is a fund or organization established and maintained for the purpose of supporting an institution or a cause. **LO 4-2**

    10. ____

Part 2 Multiple Choice

Directions: In the Answers column, write the letter that represents the word, or group of words, that correctly completes the statement or answers the question.

Answers

11. Which of the following statements about IRAs is *correct*? (a) All IRAs are insured up to $250,000. (b) IRAs must be set up at banks. (c) Many IRAs are invested in stocks and mutual funds. (d) You can put an unlimited amount of money into an IRA every year. **LO 4-1**

    11. ____

12. You can begin withdrawing money from your IRA at age _____; you *must* begin withdrawing money from the account at age _____. (a) 59 1/2; 70 1/2 (b) 59 1/2; 65 (c) 65; 70 1/2 (d) 65; 75 **LO 4-1**

    12. ____

13. This is a tax-deferred retirement plan for small business owners and their employees. (a) traditional IRA (b) Roth IRA (c) SEP IRA (d) Super IRA **LO 4-1**

    13. ____

14. Of the following, who is *most* likely to open a Keogh account? (a) Ashish, a programmer for Microsoft (b) Rusty, who runs his own lawn-mowing business (c) Natasha, a teacher in a large public high school (d) Amber, a self-employed pediatrician **LO 4-1**

    14. ____

15. An annuity _____. (a) is a contract purchased from a savings and loan (b) guarantees a series of regular monthly payments for a set period of time (c) is insured by the FDIC (d) all of these **LO 4-1**

    15. ____

16. This is a tax-deferred retirement plan funded by employees of government and nonprofit organizations. (a) Keogh plan (b) 401(k) plan (c) 403(b) plan (d) Roth IRA **LO 4-1**   16. ____

17. You should start your retirement and estate planning when _____. (a) you turn age 50 (b) you have children (c) you get married (d) you start your first career **LO 4-2**   17. ____

18. A(n) _____ is all that a person owns less debt owed at the time of the person's death? (a) estate (b) inheritance (c) legacy (d) trust **LO 4-2**   18. ____

19. This is a handwritten document that declares your wishes after your death. (a) simple will (b) holographic will (c) trust will (d) valid will **LO 4-2**   19. ____

20. This is a form of charitable giving that supports some type of societal purpose over an extended period of time. (a) benefaction (b) philanthropy (c) patronage (d) sponsorship **LO 4-2**   20. ____

Part 3 Short Answer

Directions: Read the following questions, and write your response.

21. A major advantage of many retirement plans is that they are *tax-deferred*. What does this mean? **LO 4-1**

22. What does it mean to become *vested* in a retirement plan? **LO 4-1**

23. What is *probate*? **LO 4-2**

Part 4 Critical Thinking

Directions: Read the following questions, and write your response.

24. Explain the difference between a defined-benefit plan and a defined-contribution plan. **LO 4-1**

25. What are some expenses that will probably go down for you when you retire? What expenses will stay the same? Will any expenses go up after you retire? **LO 4-2**

Chapter 17 Review

Part 1 True or False

Directions: Place a *T* for True or an *F* for False in the Answers column to show whether each of the following statements is true or false.

Answers

1. *Inflation risk* is the chance that the rate of inflation will grow more slowly than the rate of return on your investment. **LO 1-1**

   1._____

2. *Dollar-cost averaging* is a technique where you buy stocks at a low price and sell them at a high price. **LO 1-1**

   2._____

3. Indirect investing lowers your investment risk. **LO 1-2**

   3._____

4. Investors in bonds are taking less risk; thus, the return is also lower. **LO 2-1**

   4._____

5. An *agency bond* is a municipal bond that is backed by the power of the issuing state or local government to levy taxes that will pay back the debt. **LO 2-2**

   5._____

6. Real estate is often considered a good long-term investment. **LO 3-1**

   6._____

7. Silver coins are often worth up to 500 times their face value. **LO 3-2**

   7._____

8. Money withdrawn from an IRA before age 59 1/2 is subject to regular tax rates plus a 10 percent early withdrawal penalty. **LO 4-1**

   8._____

9. The person who represents you in administering your will is called the executor. **LO 4-2**

   9._____

10. Philanthropy is the primary source of funding for the fine arts, the performing arts, and most religious and humanitarian causes. **LO 4-2**

   10._____

Part 2 Multiple Choice

Directions: In the Answers column, write the letter that represents the word, or group of words, that correctly completes the statement or answers the question.

Answers

11. Which of these is an example of direct investing? (a) purchasing mutual funds (b) purchasing stocks from individual companies (c) joining an investment club (d) all of these **LO 1-1**

   11._____

12. A(n) _____ invests in international companies and new industries in foreign countries. (a) global fund (b) index fund (c) new venture fund (d) precious metals fund **LO 1-2**

   12._____

13. This type of bond, often called a mortgage bond, is backed by specific assets. (a) junk bond (b) debenture (c) secured bond (d) serial bond **LO 2-1**

   13._____

14. A convertible bond _____. (a) usually costs more than other types of bonds (b) can be exchanged for shares of stock at a preset date or within a preset period of time (c) has a variable rate of return (d) can be paid off at a preset date or within a preset period of time **LO 2-1**

   14._____

15. This type of bond is issued by state or local governments. (a) savings bond (b) agency bond (c) municipal bond (d) treasury bond **LO 2-2**

   15._____

16. Purchasing rental property _____. (a) would not usually be considered a speculative investment (b) can be financed at a very favorable rate if the income-producing potential is documented (c) rarely requires a large down payment of cash (d) all of these **LO 3-1**

   16._____

17. The right to buy shares of stock at a set price before an expiration date is called a(n) _____. (a) exchange-traded option (b) put option (c) dealer option (d) call option **LO 3-2**   17._____

18. This is an individual retirement account that allows individuals to contribute pre-tax income to an account that grows tax-deferred. (a) Roth IRA (b) Keogh account (c) traditional IRA (d) annuity **LO 4-1**   18._____

19. A 401(k) plan is a type of _____. (a) defined-contribution plan (b) annuity (c) defined-benefit plan (d) traditional IRA **LO 4-1**   19._____

20. People who will inherit your property from you are called your _____. (a) beneficiaries (b) heirs (c) successors (d) executors **LO 4-2**   20._____

Part 3 Short Answer

Directions: Read the following questions, and write your response.

21. Compare and contrast *equity financing* and *debt financing*. **LO 1-1/LO 2-1**

22. What is a *living will*? **LO 4-2**

Part 4 Critical Thinking

Directions: Read the following question, and write your response.

23. Comic books and baseball cards are examples of items that were once considered "kid stuff" but are now valuable collectible items. What are some "worthless" objects you believe might become valuable collectible items in the future? Explain your answer. **LO 3-2**